short break **tours**

Lakes and Dales

Published by VisitBritain

Published by VisitBritain Publishing
Thames Tower, Blacks Road, London W6 9EL

First published 2007

Maps reproduced by kind permission of Ordnance Survey on behalf of HMSO.
© Crown copyright 2007. All rights reserved. Ordnance Survey Licence number
100040235.

ISBN 978 0 7095 8400 1
Product code: SBTR01

A CIP catalogue record for this book is available from the British Library.

Produced for VisitBritain Publishing by Departure Lounge Limited
Contributing authors: Lindsay Hunt, Terry Marsh
Cartography: Cosmographics (pages 8–9); Draughtsman Maps
Reprographics by Blaze Creative
Printed and bound in the UK by Stones The Printers

Jacket: Main image: Derwent Water, Keswick, Cumbria
Top inset image: Rievaulx Abbey, North Yorkshire
Bottom inset image: Ashness Bridge, Cumbria
Title page: Sheep, Yorkshire Dales
pages 4–5: Lake and mountains at twilight, Cumbria

Contents

Lakes and Dales

From the lonely beauty of moorlands and dales to glistening lakes reflecting soaring mountain peaks, our tours lead you through stunning landscapes and into the heart of historic cities. Spend a day within York's city walls, clamber over castle ruins and explore quaint villages or simply soak up the stunning scenery of some of England's best-loved National Parks. The mountains of Cumbria and the wild moors and rolling dales of Yorkshire have long been the haunt of writers and poets, so seek out their homes and wander at will in the beautiful countryside that inspired them.

Specialist travel writers have crafted the 10 guided driving tours in this book to cover circular routes of two to four days, which include famous and lesser-known sights alike. The itineraries can be joined at any point along the way or easily linked to shape a longer journey and, where appropriate, each itinerary also suggests ways to extend your trip with scenic walks, tours on heritage railways and boat trips.

A PROMISE OF QUALITY

We have not included specific details in this guide of places to stay on your short break in England, but you will find a wide choice of places to stay across the region. Choosing somewhere displaying the Enjoy England Quality Rose ensures you know what to expect and can book with confidence.

The following tourist board websites will provide you with detailed information on where you can stay and eat in the areas covered by this guide, as well as other useful travel advice.

www.enjoyengland.com
www.visitbritain.com
www.visitenglandsnorthwest.com
www.yorkshirevisitor.com
www.golakes.co.uk

The Tours

This guide contains a selection of special driving itineraries plotted on detailed maps. These circular routes can be joined at any point to explore as many places each day as you wish. The short descriptions highlight places of interest within each tour whilst tinted boxes feature information on related people, events and stories. A final box also suggests places off the route that are worth a detour. Remember, it is also a good idea to makes use of available park-and-ride schemes for popular places and attractions.

Introduction
Each tour has a short introduction that gives a flavour of the area covered by the tour route.

Tour map
Each route is plotted on the tour map in blue. Blue numbered bullets correspond to the number of each entry and the name is labelled in blue. Places mentioned in the 'with more time' box are also labelled in blue – and where located off the map, are arrowed off.

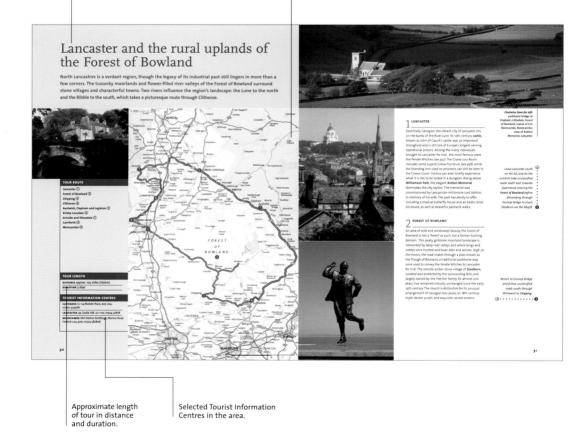

Approximate length of tour in distance and duration.

Selected Tourist Information Centres in the area.

Overleaf you will find a simple map of the region showing the location of all the tours. Each has been cross-referenced to page so you can turn straight to your chosen itinerary. In each case, the start of the tour is clearly marked by a light grey circle.

Directions
A suggested route between consecutive entries is provided. You might also like to use a full road atlas to check minor roads.

Feature boxes
The story behind selected places; literary and historical links; local legends and heroes; or suggested walks and cycle rides.

Leave Silverdale east by following signs for Yealand Redmayne, and in the village turn onto the A6 south and follow the road to Carnforth.

7 ARNSIDE AND SILVERDALE

Located in an Area of Outstanding Natural Beauty, the seaside town of **Arnside** looks out across the Kent Estuary and the hills of the southern Lake District beyond. From the wooded hill of Arnside Knott and the neighbouring village of **Silverdale** to the south, there are unrivalled views of the vast spread of Morecambe Bay. There are lovely walks out of Silverdale to the headland of Jack Scout, owned mostly by the National Trust.

Nearby, **Leighton Moss Nature Reserve** is a vast and popular nature reserve with some rare species of breeding birds among the many thousands that flock to its wetlands. Above the reserve stands the stately neogothic **Leighton Hall**, owned and lived in by the descendants of the furniture-making Gillow dynasty as it has been for centuries. Consequently, the house has all the atmosphere of a family home, and visitors are invited to sit on the ancient chairs while knowledgeable guides reveal the hall's history. You are even welcome to take your place at the 18th-century dining table or to play a tune on the Steinway. As well as landscaped parkland and woodland walks, Leighton has a pretty 19th-century walled garden – the passion of the present owner – featuring rose-covered walls, a fragrant herb patch and an overflowing herbaceous border.

Take the A6 south through Bolton-le-Sands, eventually branching right onto the A5105 for 3 miles to reach Morecambe.

8 CARNFORTH

This small Victorian market town is always busy and gains all the breezy benefits of its location on the edge of Morecambe Bay. But its fame rests on the fact that in 1945 *Brief Encounter*, starring Celia Johnson and Trevor Howard, was filmed in Carnforth **station**. The film is a love story about a man and a woman, both married but not to each other, who meet in the refreshment room at a railway station. Carnforth station cafe is now a nostalgic spot for film buffs. The town also offers some nice walks along the River Keer, the bay and the Lancaster Canal.

THE GILLOWS OF LEIGHTON HALL

The Lancaster branch of the Gillows family has been making furniture as well as architectural joinery and billiard tables, encouraged by the game's vogue, since the 1770s. The Gillows were shrewd in producing a neat, rather conventional range of furniture derived from the designs of James Wyatt, the most fashionable architect of the last two decades of the 18th century, and from plates in the pattern-books of George Hepplewhite and Thomas Sheraton. They avoided the height of fashion, supplying instead pieces that would appeal to the burgeoning middle classes of Liverpool and Manchester, who valued good, solid, well-made furniture.

Clockwise from top right:
Morecambe Bay;
Leighton Hall

9 MORECAMBE

In the early 19th century, Morecambe was simply a small fishing village called Poulton-le-Sands, but it blossomed into one of the most attractive and popular holiday resorts in Lancashire. For years, there was a sense of rivalry with Blackpool, as Morecambe always had a lively character and style, one highlighted by the zany half of a famous comedy duo Morecambe and Wise. There is a lovely statue of locally born Eric Morecambe on the promenade. Another native, actress Dame Thora Hird, made her stage debut in 1911 at the age of two months when she was carried on stage at Morecambe's Royalty Theatre in a play directed by her father. The huge expanse of Morecambe Bay once offered the shortest route into Furness, or Lancashire-over-the-Sands as it was previously known. You need the company of a guide to cross safely today (see p98), but the experience is unforgettable: vast skies, a seemingly limitless sprawl of sand and river, and an awesome sense of place.

Leave Morecambe by following the B5274 east to the A589 and then take the A6 to return to Lancaster.

WITH MORE TIME

Bright, brash and breezy is the only way to describe **Blackpool** (left). A long-established holiday resort that formerly served the mill workers of Lancashire, the town now draws crowds from across Britain – anyone, really, who just wants to let their hair down for a few fun-filled days. In contrast, a short way south along the coast is Lytham – and St Anne's – two small genteel towns traditionally joined as one. Here you can enjoy the fine promenade, peaceful parks, beautiful gardens and admire the town's old half-timbered buildings.

Picture captions
A single caption describes the images on each spread; boxed images are explained in the relevant box.

Entry description
The numbered entries explore some of the area's key attractions.

With more time box
This offers suggestions for places and attractions that are off the route but worth exploring if you have more time.

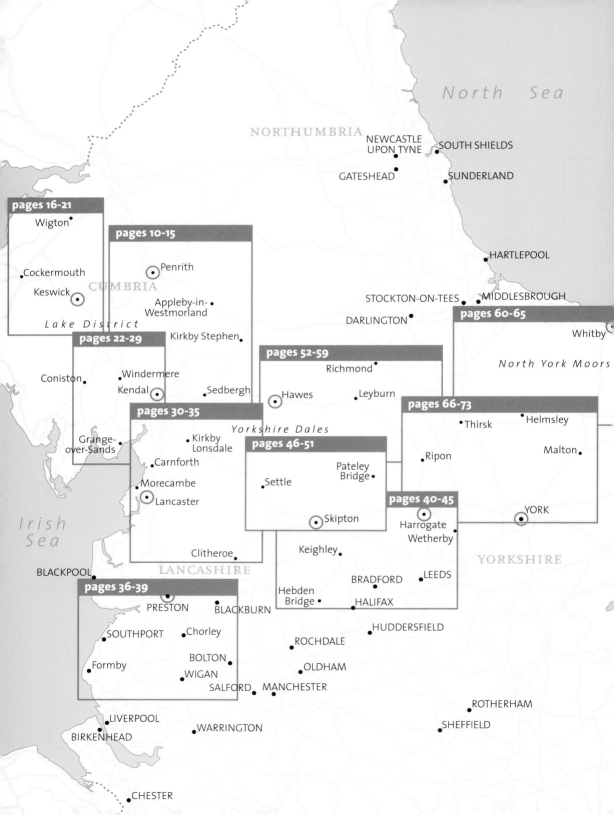

North Sea

NORTHUMBRIA

NEWCASTLE UPON TYNE
SOUTH SHIELDS
GATESHEAD
SUNDERLAND

HARTLEPOOL

STOCKTON-ON-TEES
MIDDLESBROUGH
DARLINGTON

pages 16-21
Wigton

pages 10-15

Cockermouth
Keswick

CUMBRIA

Penrith

Appleby-in-Westmorland

Kirkby Stephen

Lake District

pages 22-29

Coniston

Windermere
Kendal
Sedbergh

pages 60-65
Whitby

North York Moors

pages 52-59

Richmond

Hawes
Leyburn

pages 66-73
Thirsk
Helmsley

Grange-over-Sands

pages 30-35

Yorkshire Dales

Kirkby Lonsdale
Carnforth

Morecambe
Lancaster

pages 46-51

Settle

Pateley Bridge

Skipton

Ripon
Malton

pages 40-45

Harrogate
Wetherby
YORK

YORKSHIRE

Irish Sea

Clitheroe

LANCASHIRE

BLACKPOOL

pages 36-39

PRESTON
BLACKBURN

SOUTHPORT
Chorley

Formby
BOLTON
WIGAN
SALFORD
MANCHESTER

Keighley

Hebden Bridge
BRADFORD
LEEDS
HALIFAX

HUDDERSFIELD

ROCHDALE
OLDHAM

LIVERPOOL
WARRINGTON
BIRKENHEAD

ROTHERHAM
SHEFFIELD

CHESTER

THE TOURS

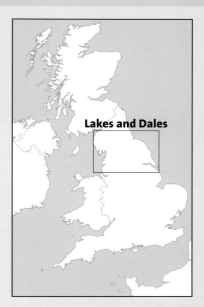

Lakes and Dales

KINGSTON UPON HULL

GRIMSBY

NCOLN

Miles 0   50

Kms 0   50

The dramatic hills and dales of eastern Lakeland

The pastoral land of the eastern Lakes, fed largely by the meandering River Eden, was once part of the ancient counties of Cumberland and Westmorland. It is the bedrock of ancient kingdoms, stories of legendary giants, Arthurian mythology and valiant knights. Castles and busy market towns huddle below the highest of the Pennine mountains, and small lakeside settlements fringe Ullswater.

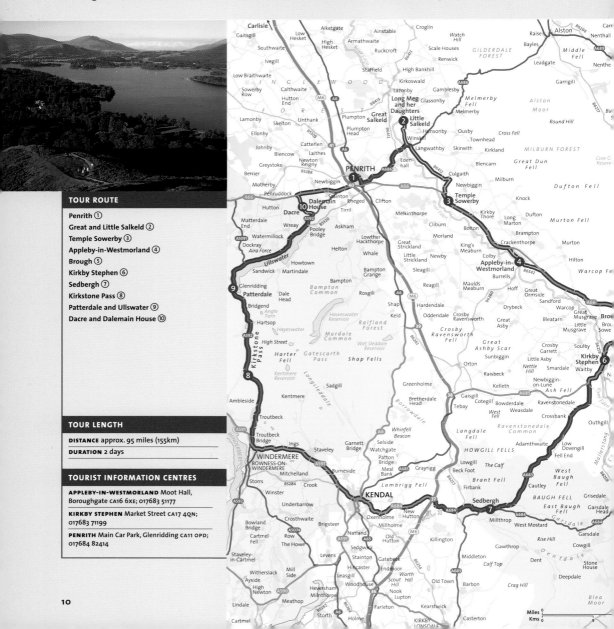

TOUR ROUTE

- Penrith ①
- Great and Little Salkeld ②
- Temple Sowerby ③
- Appleby-in-Westmorland ④
- Brough ⑤
- Kirkby Stephen ⑥
- Sedbergh ⑦
- Kirkstone Pass ⑧
- Patterdale and Ullswater ⑨
- Dacre and Dalemain House ⑩

TOUR LENGTH

DISTANCE approx. 95 miles (155km)

DURATION 2 days

TOURIST INFORMATION CENTRES

APPLEBY-IN-WESTMORLAND Moot Hall, Boroughgate CA16 6XE; 017683 51177

KIRKBY STEPHEN Market Street CA17 4QN; 017683 71199

PENRITH Main Car Park, Glenridding CA11 0PD; 017684 82414

Clockwise from far left:
Ullswater lake; Ullswater village; Martindale, near Ullswater; daffodils at Ullswater; River Eden

1 PENRITH

Penrith is a bustling market town, and around its market place is a labyrinth of lanes, yards and alleyways leading to attractive cottages, gardens and curious specialist shops. The town is built largely of local red sandstone, the same material that was used to build **Penrith Castle** in 1399, when William Strickland (later the Archbishop of Canterbury) extended an earlier pele tower. The castle was improved and added to over the next 70 years, and became a royal fortress for Richard, Duke of Gloucester, later King Richard III. High above the town is **Penrith Beacon**, built in 1719 on a spot where beacons have been lit in times of war and emergency since the days of Henry VIII. You can walk up to the beacon, from where there is an invigorating view across the Eden Valley to the Lakeland hills. On the outskirts of town, housed in Britain's largest earth-covered building, lies **Rheged – The Village in the Hill**, a place of art, craft, local culture and history. Among the attractions in this subterranean world are an IMAX cinema screen the size of six double-decker buses, which shows films of world exploration from the Grand Canyon to Everest. An exhibit showcasing British mountaineering illustrates how Britain's great mountaineers tackled the world's highest summits.

*Leave Penrith on the A686 to Langwathby. Follow unclassified roads to **Little Salkeld**. Park in the village and walk up to Long Meg and her Daughters.* **2**

2 GREAT AND LITTLE SALKELD

The villages of Great and Little Salkeld face each other across the River Eden, the 'little' linked to the 'great' only by bridges at Lazonby, to the north, and Langwathby, to the south. They are worth seeking out for the standing stones known as **Long Meg and her Daughters**, mute witnesses to the whole history of man in the Eden Valley. Unlike many stone circles, Long Meg and her family survived the anti-pagan fervour of the 18th century. Legend has it that they are witches turned to stone by the 13th-century magician Michael Scott for holding orgies and dancing on the sabbath. A short walk away are **Lacy's Caves**, created by Colonel Lacy, the 18th-century owner of Salkeld Hall. Quite why, is not clear, though it was more than likely in pursuit of the fashion of the time to build 'antiquities' and 'romantic' caves.

*Return south to the A686 and turn left and shortly right onto the B6412, going south east through Culgaith to reach Acorn Bank at **Temple Sowerby**.*
 3

Clockwise from above:
Acorn Bank; view from
Kirkstone Pass;
Kirkby Stephen

3 TEMPLE SOWERBY

A pleasant, neat and attractive village of Georgian
houses centred around a large green, Temple Sowerby
was owned by the Knights Templar and later the
Knights Hospitaller until the Dissolution under Henry
VIII. Among the lovely buildings here is **Acorn Bank**, a
fine 18th-century manor house, and former home of
Dorothy Ratcliffe, who wrote in the Yorkshire dialect. In
the sheltered garden, surrounded by ancient oak trees,
there is a captivating display of herbaceous borders,
roses and flowering shrubs. The herb garden here is
renowned for the largest collection of medicinal and
culinary plants in the north of England, and there's also
a pleasing woodland walk beside Crowdundle Beck to
the watermill, which is open to visitors.

⊕ Take the A66 south east for
• 6 miles, and then branch
• right onto the B6542 into
④ *Appleby-in-Westmorland.*

4 APPLEBY-IN-WESTMORLAND

Formerly the county town of Westmorland, Appleby is a
market town of great character. It is divided by the
River Eden into two parts: old Appleby around St
Michael's church and new Appleby centred around
Boroughgate, a fine high street flanked by lime trees
and attractive red sandstone houses that give the town
a mellow, warm appearance. Appleby is overlooked by
its imposing Norman **castle**, located on a steep bank
above the river. Largely restored and rebuilt in the 17th
century, it is surrounded by moats that define an inner
and at least two outer baileys. Today, Appleby is most
renowned for its lively horse fair (*see box*).

⊕ Continue south east along
• the B6542 and rejoin the
⑤ A66 to **Brough.**

*Leave Brough heading
south on the A685 for 4
miles to **Kirkby Stephen.***

→ • • • • • • • • • • ⑥

5 BROUGH

Brough (pronounced 'Bruff') comprises Market Brough,
Church Brough and Brough Sowerby. Church Brough is
a collection of stone houses centred around a village
green. Market Brough, where a market cross tops a
clock tower, grew around a 14th-century bridge
spanning Swindale Beck; and Brough Sowerby lies one
mile to the south. Located on the important
stagecoach routes from London to Carlisle and
Glasgow, and from York to Lancaster, the town
prospered during the 18th and 19th centuries,
employing a large number of stable boys, ostlers, cooks,
innkeepers, blacksmiths and wheelwrights to service
the needs of travellers. The ruins of a Norman **castle**
stand in a dominant position above the river, and
occupy the northern part of the site of the Roman fort
of Verterae of which nothing remains. As at Appleby,
each September sees an annual gathering of Romany
people who come to Brough Hill Fair, an event that has
taken place for the past 600 years.

6 KIRKBY STEPHEN

In response to continuous border raids, the old market town of Kirkby Stephen is a maze of narrow, high-walled passages and spacious squares into which cattle could be driven in times of trouble. The central market square is surrounded by a ring of cobblestones that demarcate the area used until 1820 for bull baiting. Just off the square, the church of **St Stephen's**, known locally as the Cathedral of the Dales, bears traces of Saxon and Norman handiwork, and Dalesfolk have worshipped on this site for over 1,500 years. It contains the 8th-century Viking **Loki Stone**. Named after a Norse god, it depicts a bound devil and is one of only two such stones in Europe. Kirkby Stephen is a staging post for walkers undertaking the Coast-to-Coast Walk. There is also an easy, uphill moorland walk from the town to Nine Standards Rigg on the Cumbrian border.

Dotted around the Eden Valley landscape are a number of carved stone sculptures, which double as seats. Part of a millennium scheme, they are known as 'Eden Benchmarks'. If you're not expecting them they can take you quite by surprise, but they offer delightful spots to sit quietly and contemplate the landscape. In Kirkby Stephen itself you'll also find a number of sculpted stones along a 'Poetry Path', which was devised to highlight the landscape of the Eden Valley.

7 SEDBERGH

The small, stone-built town of Sedbergh became part of Cumbria in 1974, even though it clearly has many 'Dales' affinities: it is in fact located in the Yorkshire Dales National Park and its western gateway. An ancient market town, its fame rests on the laurels of Sedbergh School, set in parkland on the edge of town. Among its memorable pupils was Will Carling, former captain of the England rugby team. To the north of town rise the rounded Howgills, a fine and compact group of fells that provide excellent walking country.

8 KIRKSTONE PASS

Rising from the urban sprawl of Windermere, a long and winding road climbs through the increasingly austere landscape to Kirkstone Pass, a long-established route into Patterdale. In winter, the 457-m pass (1490-ft) can become blocked with snow, but at any time it is a wild place, and takes its name from a nearby boulder that has the rough outline of a church, or 'kirk'.

*Continue south on A685, and then branch left onto A683 to **Sedbergh**.* **7**

*Take the A684 west to Kendal and drive through the town to join the A591 for Windermere. Stay on the A591 until you can branch right onto the A592 north for **Kirkstone Pass**.* **8**

*Continue over Kirkstone Pass and descend via Hartsop to **Patterdale** and **Ullswater**. Continue north east up the dale to pass the junction with A5091, and reach Aira Force.* **9**

9 PATTERDALE AND ULLSWATER

Patterdale may be named after St Patrick, one of three missionaries thought to have travelled in this region during the 5th century. Located at the southern end of Ullswater, the village, buttressed by high fells, was described by Baddeley in his *Guide to the English Lake District* as 'one of the most charmingly situated in Britain, and in itself clean and comely'. Many of these remote villages were presided over by one dominant family. In Patterdale it was the Mounseys, who were described as the 'kings of Patterdale', and lived at **Patterdale Hall**, now rebuilt, but dating from around 1677. Nearby, the grounds around the impressive waterfall of **Aira Force** are now owned by the National Trust, and are a prime example of a landscaped Victorian park.

Many regard Ullswater as the most beautiful lake in the region. Its gently curving shape is the result of glacial action gouging out a trough 8 miles long and one mile wide, sinking to a depth of 61m (200ft). It was along the shores of Ullswater and at the foot of Gowbarrow Fell that Dorothy Wordsworth noted the daffodils that later inspired William to write his famous poem. During the summer months, you can take boat trips on the lake at Glenridding on the two recently restored 19th-century steamers *MY Raven* and *MY Lady of the Lake*, an excellent way of experiencing this stunning dale. Most walkers who come to ascend Helvellyn do so from Glenridding or nearby Patterdale by way of Striding Edge. But there are plenty of fells that offer energetic days out: Place Fell, St Sunday Crag, the valley of Grisedale and, across the lake, Martindale, one of the few places in the Lakes where red deer still abound.

*Continue on the A592 past Pooley Bridge, and take the turning left to **Dacre**. If visiting **Dalemain**, return to the A592 and turn left where signposted a little further on.*

LADY ANNE CLIFFORD

Lady Anne Clifford, who lies buried in the churchyard in Appleby, was a remarkable woman. The daughter of George Clifford, 3rd Earl of Cumberland and a naval commander, she was born in Skipton in 1590. She inherited the Clifford estates in 1643, at the time of the Civil War, and moved north. She then became a royalist thorn in Cromwell's side, frequently defying his express orders and rebuilding and restoring her castles at Appleby, Bardon Tower, Brough, Brougham, Pendragon and Skipton. Lady Anne's influence was felt throughout these northern parts of England, and many buildings in the area, particularly churches, are well-restored due to her dedication and determination.

Clockwise from far left:
Patterdale; Ullswater

10   DACRE AND DALEMAIN HOUSE

A little off the beaten track, the village of Dacre is a gem. The name is derived from the Welsh for tear, *daigr*, though there is nothing to be sad about in this quiet village set in splendid isolation along the crystal waters of Dacre Beck. On the site of a Saxon monastery, it is believed to have been here that pagan kings swore allegiance to Aethelstan, and were baptised into Christianity. At the four corners of the churchyard stand the enigmatic **Dacre Bears**, four large stone sculptures, now largely weathered, and thought to commemorate the marriage between Thomas de Dacre and Philippa Neville, though their true origin is unknown. The monuments seem to depict an encounter between a bear and a cat: one shows the bear sleeping, then the cat awakens the bear, which seizes the cat, kills it and promptly eats it.

In the lakeland fells east of Dacre stands **Dalemain House**, a mainly 18th-century mansion that was built around an earlier house and a Norman pele tower. It was purchased in 1680 by Sir Edward Hasell, the son of the rector of Middleton Cheney in Northamptonshire, and has remained in the same family ever since. The interior features marvellous oak work, mostly originating from the estate, and portraits by van Dyck, bequeathed by Lady Anne Clifford (*see p14*), adorn the walls. The gardens have flourished since the 12th century, but today the real floral treat is the May to June display of Himalayan Blue poppies that thrive here.

*Join the A66 north of Dacre or Dalemain to return east to **Penrith***

WITH MORE TIME

The border city of **Carlisle**, once a crucible of murder, mischief and mayhem, is now the administrative centre of Cumbria, and worth a detour. The medieval fortress of Carlisle castle sits squarely at the heart of the city. The simplicity of the building contrasts hugely with the stone filigree Victorian adornment that adorns Carlisle's mainly 19th-century cathedral. The modern red-brick Tullie House Musem and Art Gallery hosts regular exhibitions and permanent displays reflecting the Roman and Reiver history of the city and border area.

The rugged fells of western Lakeland

Beyond the high road passes such as Honister and Hard Knott, the landscape of western Lakeland becomes more rugged and austere. Keswick, the largest town in the Lake District, is the gateway to this part of western England where sights include neat Cumbrian villages and craggy fells that brood over magnificent lakes and vales, vestiges of the ice age when creeping glaciers gouged out the landscape. Today, this remote area retains an originality, a touch of 'otherness' that both intrigues and attracts.

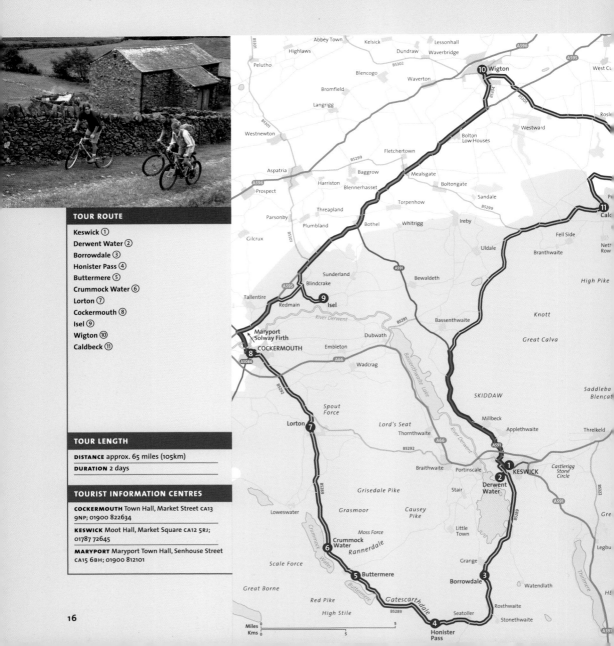

TOUR ROUTE

Keswick ①
Derwent Water ②
Borrowdale ③
Honister Pass ④
Buttermere ⑤
Crummock Water ⑥
Lorton ⑦
Cockermouth ⑧
Isel ⑨
Wigton ⑩
Caldbeck ⑪

TOUR LENGTH

DISTANCE approx. 65 miles (105km)
DURATION 2 days

TOURIST INFORMATION CENTRES

COCKERMOUTH Town Hall, Market Street CA13 9NP; 01900 822634

KESWICK Moot Hall, Market Square CA12 5RJ; 01787 72645

MARYPORT Maryport Town Hall, Senhouse Street CA15 6BH; 01900 812101

1 KESWICK

Centered on its bustling market place, Keswick is the pretty 'capital' of Western Lakeland. The town's superb setting at the head of Derwent Water at the northern end of Borrowdale, arguably Lakeland's most beautiful valley, makes it a big centre for fell walkers, climbers and holiday makers.

Built from local Skiddaw slate, Keswick's handsome buildings line its winding streets. The Moot Hall (now the tourist information centre) was built in 1813 on the site of an earlier building and, even until fairly recently, was used as the town hall. Keswick grew in importance from Elizabethan times, when it became a prosperous mining centre: as well as copper and lead, graphite was mined in the Borrowdale fells, and from the late 1800s pencils were manufactured locally in factories. The **Cumberland Pencil Museum** tells the story of pencils from the discovery of graphite to present-day methods of manufacture. Four miles north of Keswick along the shores of Bassenthwaite lake stands the 17th-century **Mirehouse**, which had strong literary connections, being visited by Southey, Tennyson and Wordsworth. It was during Tennyson's stay here that he was moved to write a poem describing the passing of King Arthur, later published as part of *Idylls of the King*.

On the fells just to the south east of town, **Castlerigg Stone Circle** enjoys a dramatic setting and is believed to date from 3000 BC, older than the great circles at Stonehenge and Avebury. It is commonly regarded as Cumbria's most superb stone circle.

Clockwise from far left: cyclists near Keswick; mists over Derwent Water; Borrowdale; walkers on Cat Bells; Castlerigg Stone Circle; Ashness Bridge, near Keswick

*Leave Keswick following signs to the B5289. Head south in the direction of Borrowdale: **Derwent Water** lies to your right.*

➡ • • • • • • • • • ❷

⊕ *Continue along the B5289*
• *into Borrowdale, past the*
• *bridge at Grange. Just over*
• *one mile further on, keep*
• *an eye open for the parking*
❸ *place for the Bowder Stone.*

2 DERWENT WATER

From the popular water's-edge viewpoint of Friar's Crag, the view over Derwent Water and into the hazy blue-green depths of Borrowdale is quite stunning. On a calm day, the brackeny slopes of Cat Bells and Maiden Moor are faithfully mirrored in the lake offering two spectacular images for the price of one. There are four islands in the lake, and one that early writers believed to be a floating island – in reality a mass of submerged vegetation that appears when the water level is low. In the late 1700s the eccentric Joseph Pocklington, known as Lord Pocky, lived on the largest island, **Derwent Isle**. Considered a man who never understood the concept of restraint, he built several picturesque extravaganzas on his island, including a chapel and a Druid's Circle, though only the chapel remains today.

One of the least taxing and most enjoyable ways of appreciating lower Borrowdale is to join a boat cruise on Derwent Water. The launches start their journey from the Keswick boat landings and cruise around the lake stopping at seven different jetties. You can start or break your journey at any of these, and pick up a later boat to resume the tour; the round trip takes 50 minutes.

3 BORROWDALE

The valley of Borrowdale is staggeringly beautiful, many of its tree-cloaked sides looking now much as they would have before man appeared. As you look south towards Grange, the valley seems blocked by a huge wooded crag named Castle Crag. But there is a way past the so-called tooth in the 'Jaws of Borrowdale'. A wooded path and the valley road follow the River Derwent and are flanked on both sides by high fells, which offer a network of routes for walkers.

Concealed high above the Borrowdale valley, the ancient hamlet of **Watendlath** was used by writer Hugh Walpole (who lived locally from 1924 to 1941), as his setting for *Judith Paris*, one of his *Rogue Herries* titles; Foldhead Farm in Watendlath is thought to be the model for Rogue Herries Farm. Then, as now, the hamlet is remote and unspoilt, a cluster of whitewashed cottages beside a trout-laden tarn that is popular with anglers.

No one seems quite sure whether the **Bowder Stone** near the hamlet of Grange, and easily accessible by constructed pathways, fell from the crags above or was left by a retreating glacier. The name comes from the Middle English 'bulder-stan', meaning a large boulder. Nearby is a small cottage built by Joseph Pocklington as a home for a local guide. In the base of the boulder, reputed to weigh about 2,000 tons, is a small hole, also the responsibility of Pocklington, who created it so that visitors could shake hands through it with their guide.

Keep on the B5289, passing
through Rosthwaite to
Seatoller. The road will then
climb very steeply to the
top of the Honister Pass.

➔ • • • • • • • • • • ❹

Clockwise from far left:
Derwent Water; Buttermere

THE MAID OF BUTTERMERE

In the early 19th century, Buttermere's Fish Hotel was kept by a couple called Robinson who had a stunningly beautiful daughter, Mary. When only 14, Mary was remarked upon by Captain Budworth in his book *A Fortnight's Ramble in the Lakes*, and she became something of a local celebrity as the 'Beauty of Buttermere'. When she was 24, Mary caught the eye of a personable visitor to Buttermere, the Honourable Alexander Augustus Hope, Lieutenant-Colonel in the 14th Regiment of Foot. The colonel wooed and won the Beauty of Buttermere, and they were married in Lorton church in 1802. Ironically, poet Coleridge, a long-standing admirer of Mary, wrote a piece on the wedding for the *Morning Post*, where it eventually came to the notice of the genuine Colonel Hope, who had been abroad all that summer, for Mary's husband was an impostor. Local broadcaster and writer Lord Melvyn Bragg published a popular novel based on the story in 1987.

4 HONISTER PASS

The onward route through Borrowdale passes through the village of **Seatoller** (one of the wettest places in England), and up to Honister Pass 356m (1168ft) above sea level. **Honister Slate Mine** is still being worked for its much-prized slate and offers guided visits into the mine. In stormy weather, Honister is a dramatic and exciting spot, and the descent into Buttermere valley is breathtaking. Long-distance walkers undertaking the Coast-to-Coast Walk pass through Honister on their way from Ennerdale to Borrowdale.

*Descend steeply into Gatescarthdale, continuing on the B5289 until the village of **Buttermere**.* **5**

5 BUTTERMERE

Throughout Buttermere the whole scene is one of nature in her most benevolent mood, for here she has bestowed great riches of scenic beauty – swelling peaks, wooded fellsides, grey crags, oases of vivid green. The poet Robert Southey wrote of Buttermere: 'The hills that, calm and majestic, lifted their heads in the silent sky… Dark and distinct they rose. The clouds have gathered above them, High in the middle air, huge, purple, pillowy masses.'

The hamlet of Buttermere, little more than two hotels and a farm, is a good base from which to tackle the easy circular walks around either Lake Buttermere or Crummock Water *(see p20)*. Experienced fell walkers may tackle the steep and friable route onto Red Pike, a superb vantage point, but it is not for the fainthearted.

*Continue on the B5289 to **Crummock Water**.*

 **6**

Clockwise from above:
Derwent Water; Wordsworth
memorial, Cockermouth;
Crummock Water

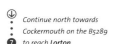

Continue north towards
Cockermouth on the B5289
⑦ to reach **Lorton**.

Head north from Lorton,
turning left on the B5292
⑧ to reach **Cockermouth**.

Take the A595, where
you turn north. Then
follow an unclassified road
to the right at Redmain
and continue to
Blindcrake. Here, turn right
until you reach the River
Derwent at Isel.

 •••••••••• ⑨

6 CRUMMOCK WATER

The larger Crummock Water is more open and less
dominated by fells than Buttermere, though the huge
bulk of Grasmoor to the north has immense presence.
It is, however, every bit as beautiful. There's a delightful
walk between **Scale Force**, the highest waterfall in the
Lake District, and the village of Buttermere across the
neck of land that links Buttermere lake and Crummock
Water. Scale Force has been a popular excursion since
Victorian times, when visitors would sail across the lake
to see it. Though a little rocky underfoot, the base of
the waterfall is nevertheless a lovely spot to have a
picnic. Also on the lake's eastern shore is **Rannerdale** –
a valley, that for all its undoubted beauty, has
something of a sinister history. It was here at the end of
the 11th century that the people of Buttermere
ambushed and slew invading Normans, leaving their
bodies to rot at the entrance to the dale. Today, this
spot bursts into an intensely bright carpet of bluebells
each spring.

7 LORTON

Two small hamlets, High and Low Lorton, combine
to create Lorton, a peaceful community of traditional
Lakeland character. John Wesley preached here
between 1752 and 1761, while 100 years earlier George
Fox, the founder of the Quaker faith, preached in High
Lorton beneath an ancient yew tree. The tree is more
than 1,000 years old, and is immortalised by
Wordsworth in his poem *Yew-Trees*.

   Lorton Hall, set apart from the hamlets near a loop
in the river, is built around a 15th-century pele tower,
though the rest of the hall dates from 1663. Charles II
stayed here in 1653, when he was out rallying support
for his cause. One of his favourite trees, the beech, was
planted by the lady of the manor, at the time of the
Restoration, and still survives. The hall is only
occasionally open to the public.

8 COCKERMOUTH

The town of Cockermouth is where William Wordsworth
and his sister Dorothy were born. Their birthplace, a
Georgian townhouse built in 1745, still stands in Main
Street. **Wordsworth House** is now a museum containing
furniture and effects of the family and the original
staircase, fireplaces and panelling. As a child,
Wordsworth played among the ruins of the 12th-
century **Cockermouth Castle** that was built with stones
from the nearby Roman settlement at Papcastle.

   The town is a bustling place with a complex and
seemingly random arrangement of lovely old cobbled
streets, alleyways and yards. The **Lakeland Sheep and
Wool Centre** on the edge of town is an excellent way of
getting to know the woolly residents of Lakeland, and
the part they played in the lives of Lakes people.

LAKELAND'S HIGHEST SUMMITS

Although there are over 200 fells in the Lake
District, few of them rise above 914m (3,000
ft), but those that do have a majesty of their
own, and each is quite distinct. In the north,
Skiddaw (*above*; 931m, 3,054ft) is composed of
slate, and has a smooth almost conical profile.
To the east, **Helvellyn** (950m, 3,116ft) has a
dramatic ice-carved, east-facing corrie, but
displays a rather plain rump to the waters of
Thirlmere. The two highest, **Scafell Pike** (978m,
3,210ft) and **Scafell** (964m, 3,162ft) stand side
by side, rugged and crag-ridden, but are
separated by a near impassable gap, forcing
walkers to descend to a rocky, scree-laden track
that rises across the north-facing cliff face of
Scafell before finally ascending to its summit.

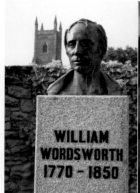

9 ISEL

Perched close to the wooded banks of the River Derwent, the tiny hamlet of Isel is notable for its squat, Norman church of **St Michael's**, built in 1130. The setting is both exquisite and typical of the times when much of Lakeland was densely wooded, and travellers resorted to the rivers and woodland tracks to move about. Places of worship were often established where routes crossed, such as at St Michael's.

Around the nearest village, **Blindcrake**, the landscape reveals an unusual Lakeland farmscape that mixes the open spaces of the ancient Isel deer park with the rarer pattern of traditional strip fields.

10 WIGTON

Wigton is an unassuming and attractive market town on the Solway Plain, with a medieval layout and much Georgian architecture. In the triangular **Market Place** is a granite fountain with a pyramid spire, and on its sides are depicted four Acts of Mercy in bronze relief. Nearby, at the end of the main street, **Wigton Hall** is neo-Tudor in design with Georgian windows. Wigton is the birthplace of Robert Smirke (1752–1845), the painter and book illustrator, as well as the renowned Cumberland poet Ewan Clark and present-day writer and broadcaster Lord Melvyn Bragg.

11 CALDBECK

Most widely renowned for its local association with 18th-century huntsman John Peel, Caldbeck is a pleasing village surrounded by farmland near the slopes of the northern Lakeland fells. The manufacture of bobbins for the mills of Lancashire was a major Lakeland industry, and the **Howk Bobbin Mill** just a short distance from the village is a relic from an era that saw many of the local rivers lined with woollen, cotton, corn, bobbin and paper mills.

The church, dedicated to **St Kentigern**, dates from the 12th century, and was restored in the 1930s. Mary, the Beauty of Buttermere *(see p19)*, who in later life was happily married to a Caldbeck man, lies buried in the churchyard, as does John Peel, the huntsman forever immortalised in the verses of *D'ye ken John Peel*, written by his friend John Woodcock Graves.

In nearby **Hesket Newmarket,** to the south east of Caldbeck, is one of the England's smallest breweries, producing a wide range of real ales.

Return to Blindcrake and turn right on the A595 for 13 miles, and then turn left on the B5304 into **Wigton**. 🔟

Take the B5305 and, at the A595, turn right and then immediately left back onto the B5305. Follow this to its junction with the B5299. There, turn right to **Caldbeck**. ⑪

Take the B5299 for 3 miles, then follow unclassified roads south west across country to reach the A591 at Bassenthwaite, and turn south towards **Keswick**.

 ❶

WITH MORE TIME

The **Solway Firth** is an atmospheric place of salt marsh and huge skies. On its southern shore, Silloth is a pretty Victorian seaside resort with a splendid promenade. It was here that J M W Turner painted his *Sunset over the Solway Firth*. Allonby has a lovely shingle and sand beach and free-roaming Allonby ponies. On the Atlantic coast, **Maryport** celebrates its maritime history with both a museum and the Maryport Steamship Museum, while the Roman occupation of north west Cumbria is the focus of the town's Senhouse Roman Museum.

The charms of southern Lakeland

The area of the southern Lake District is distinctly different from Lakeland's central, landlocked region. Here, limestone dominates the terrain, and this produces a more subtle and verdant landscape. There are few sizeable towns, but numerous villages and hamlets. There are also more wooded areas, and the weather in the south is tempered by the coastal influences from the Kent Estuary and Morecambe Bay. This is also a part of England that is well endowed with stately homes, many of which are still occupied by the same families who have lived in them for centuries.

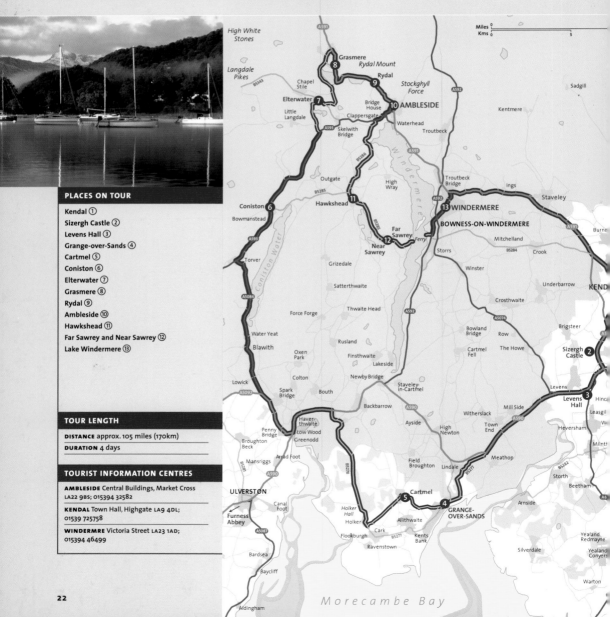

PLACES ON TOUR

Kendal ①
Sizergh Castle ②
Levens Hall ③
Grange-over-Sands ④
Cartmel ⑤
Coniston ⑥
Elterwater ⑦
Grasmere ⑧
Rydal ⑨
Ambleside ⑩
Hawkshead ⑪
Far Sawrey and Near Sawrey ⑫
Lake Windermere ⑬

TOUR LENGTH

DISTANCE approx. 105 miles (170km)
DURATION 4 days

TOURIST INFORMATION CENTRES

AMBLESIDE Central Buildings, Market Cross
LA22 9BS; 015394 32582
KENDAL Town Hall, Highgate LA9 4DL;
01539 725758
WINDERMRE Victoria Street LA23 1AD;
015394 46499

Clockwise from far left:
boats on Lake Windermere;
Lake Windermere, Cumbria;
tomb at Cartmel Priory;
Kendal Castle

1 KENDAL

Formerly an important woollen textile centre, the flourishing market town of Kendal is set amid a low-lying limestone landscape attractively crisscrossed by drystone walls and dotted with farmsteads. Today it is the southern gateway to the Lake District National Park, though the valley of the River Kent and the surrounding limestone scars offer plenty of easy walks.

Leading off Kendal's main thoroughfare is a series of parallel 'wynds' or narrow alleyways and courtyards, which developed to meet the increase in population that came with the rapid growth of the local textile industry from the 17th–19th centuries. Just outside town, **Kendal Castle** dates from the 12th century. In the 1500s, it was owned by Sir Thomas Parr, father of Katherine Parr, the last wife of Henry VIII, who was born here. It is an easy uphill walk from the banks of the River Kent and offers a splendid view over the town.

At Kendal's southern edge and housed in an imposing Georgian House, **Abbot Hall Art Gallery** has a highly acclaimed programme of contemporary exhibitions. Located in the former stables, the **Abbot Hall Museum of Lakeland Life** shows how the Cumbrian people have worked, lived and entertained themselves over the past 300 years. The adjacent church of the **Holy and Undivided Trinity** is Cumbria's largest parish church and dates from the 13th century: it is unique in having five aisles.

Leave Kendal heading south to join A591, and then follow local signs for Sizergh Castle. **2**

2 SIZERGH CASTLE

Some two miles south of Kendal stands the imposing ancestral home of the Strickland family, Sizergh Castle. The Great Hall, which was remodelled in the 1600s, and two Elizabethan wings are built around a 14th-century pele tower. Many of the rooms display a lavish use of oak panelling, and walls are decorated with family and royal portraits. There is also a collection of English and French oak furniture and fine porcelain that was acquired over the family's 750-year history. Numerous footpaths wind through the 638-ha estate (1,600 acre) to viewpoints overlooking the Kent Estuary and the fells.

Return to the A591 and head south. At the intersection with the A590 bear right and then follow local signs to Levens Hall. **3**

From Levens Hall, return to the A590 and head west for 5 miles to a roundabout and branch left on to the B5277 to Lindale. Turn left again to reach **Grange-over-Sands**.

3 LEVENS HALL

This magnificent home, owned by the same family for 700 years, was built onto an earlier pele tower. It is by far the largest Elizabethan house in the Lake District, yet has managed to keep an intimate scale. Beautiful paintings and fine panelling, plasterwork and family memorabilia adorn the rooms. The gardens and landscape that surround Levens have changed little since they were created in 1690 by Beaumont, a gardener to the aristocracy and much in demand. The topiary gardens are especially breathtaking, but don't miss the rose garden, the splendid herbaceous borders and the fountain garden with its display of ornamental limes. Part of the Levens estate is one of Cumbria's oldest deer parks, which contains some unusually dark fallow deer. Local legend has it that whenever a white fawn is born to the herd, the occasion foretells some change in the fortunes of the house of Levens.

4 GRANGE-OVER-SANDS

There is something truly relaxing about Grange-over-Sands. Situated on Morecambe Bay, its bracing sea air, mild climate and the arrival of the Furness Railway turned the former fishing village into a popular Edwardian resort. Part of its charm today is that it still retains this feel with a long, traffic-free promenade and attractive ornamental gardens. The surrounding countryside is especially appealing and popular with birdwatchers and walkers, having a wide variety of habitats.

From Grange follow the B5277 south west and then turn right using local roads to reach **Cartmel**.

Continue south west to the B5278 using local roads and head north to the junction with the A590. Turn left and then right on the A5092 and later right again onto the A5084. Continue for 6 miles to the junction with the A593 where you turn right to reach **Coniston**.

5 CARTMEL

One of south Lakeland's oldest villages, Cartmel grew up around its 12th- and 13th-century Augustinian **priory.** Much of the priory was destroyed at the time of the Dissolution, but the **church** was spared as its demolition would have left the parishioners without a place of prayer. Today, it is commonly regarded as one of Britain's most beautiful churches, and has a curious belfry set diagonally to the base of the tower. The pretty village, with its ancient streets and inviting cafes and inns is worth exploring too. The renowned Cartmel racecourse is just behind the square, with meetings held on both spring and summer bank holiday weekends.

Nearby **Holker Hall**, an attractive neo-Elizabethan mansion, is the home of Lord and Lady Cavendish. The exterior is stunning, but the interior is breathtaking in its design and decoration. Outside, part formal, part woodland gardens feature an observatory, an arboretum, terraces, a kitchen garden and a labyrinth set in a wild-flower meadow. The real highlight, though, is its **Lakeland Motor Museum**. Here, more than 20,000 cars, pedal cars and engines, tractors, motorcycles and bicycles are found in what is the most comprehensive collection of automobilia in England. For motorists, this is quite simply unadulterated nostalgia.

QUEEN'S GUIDE TO MORECAMBE BAY

The vast expanse of Morecambe Bay is no place to linger without expert guidance. There are quicksands, and the tide comes in rapidly, as many have found to their cost. Some of those who have failed to beat the tide are buried in the church grounds at Cartmel, and it was the priory that introduced the services of a guide. Today, the guide is appointed by the Queen and runs guided walks from May to September, which must be booked in advance. Attempting to walk across the bay without a guide is not recommended given the risks involved.

Clockwise from far left:
topiary at Levens Hall;
view of Coniston Water
from Nibthwaite

6 CONISTON

Dominated by the Coniston Fells, which rise to the summit of the **Old Man of Coniston** (803m, 2,634ft), this village is one of the most popular destinations in the Lake District. Almost every day of the year sees walkers setting off to climb the 'Old Man', often continuing to circle high above Goat's Water, across Dow Crag and down to the Walna Scar road. For the less energetic, walks up to Tarn Hows, across Tom Heights and onto Monk Coniston Moor offer easier circuits. The development nearby of slate quarries and copper mines in the 19th century brought Coniston much of its prosperity, but it was the beauty of both the village and its valley that attracted many: Tennyson spent part of his honeymoon here; Arthur Ransome, the writer of children's books, made Coniston the setting for *Swallows and Amazons*; W G Collingwood, the English artist and archaeologist, was a resident as was the influential poet, art critic and social reformer John Ruskin. He lived at **Brantwood**, on the shores of

Coniston Water from 1871 until his death and according to his wishes, lies buried in the local churchyard. Brantwood is one of the most beautifully situated houses in the Lakes, enjoying stunning views. During Ruskin's time here, it became one of the greatest literary and artistic centres in Europe. Today Brantwood houses a museum commemorating his life and work.

Five mile-long **Coniston Water** was the setting for Donald Campbell's ill-fated attempt at the world jet-powered water-speed record in 1967. His boat, *Bluebird*, went out of control as he attempted to become the first man to exceed 300mph on water, and Campbell was killed. His death is commemorated in the village centre by a plaque. Before the advent of the automobile, Coniston Water was immensely popular with visitors who would arrive by rail. The Furness Railway Company also operated a steamer service on the lake: first launched in 1859, after years of disuse, *The Gondola* was rebuilt and brought back into service in 1980.

*Continue north east on
the A593 and after about
5 miles turn left along local
roads to **Elterwater**.*

7 ELTERWATER

Standing at the entrance to Langdale, and with the craggy Langdale Pikes as a backdrop, Elterwater is a delightful cluster of attractive cottages, shops and an inn. The name of the village is said to mean 'swan lake' in Norse, and swans still grace the nearby Elterwater from time to time. Surrounded by waterfalls, volcanic crags and tree-clad slopes offering plenty of fell walking opportunities, the village is largely built of the attractive, local grey-green slate, and centres on a small green with an ancient maple tree. The manufacture of gunpowder came to be an important Lakeland industry during the 18th century, and the gunpowder works at Elterwater, responsible for the development of the village, did not close until the 1930s.

Head north to reach
the junction with the
B5343. Take unclassified
roads to the A591
8 and **Grasmere**.

8 GRASMERE

Associated forever with the poet William Wordsworth, and a tourist magnet as a consequence, Grasmere is nevertheless a delightful settlement located in a vast natural hollow at the foot of the steady rise to Dunmail Raise. Fells of varying heights and steepness enfold the village, and provide by far the best view of it, while the nearby lake of Grasmere adds a certain sparkle.

Dove Cottage, where the Wordsworths lived, was originally an inn called the Dove and Olive Bough. In Wordsworth's time it had no name, however, and was simply looked on as part of Town End, a small hamlet. The Wordsworths repaired and decorated the cottage themselves, and it was here that Dorothy, his sister, kept her *Journals*, written between 1800 and 1803, an almost daily account of the goings-on in their lives. Today, the cottage receives thousands of visitors annually, who come to see the miscellaneous household items, furniture, possessions and portraits from the poet's day, and to wander the small garden that William and Dorothy created. Wordsworth is buried in a quiet corner of the churchyard of St Oswald, along with Mary, his wife; Dorothy, his sister; and three of his children, Dora, Catherine and Thomas. The grave shelters beneath one of eight yew trees planted in the churchyard by the poet.

Immediately adjoining the church is the renowned **Grasmere Gingerbread Shop**, built in 1660 and formerly the village school. It was attended by the Wordsworth children when the family lived at the Rectory (1811–13) and was eventually taken over by a 19th-century entrepreneur, Sarah Nelson, who made gingerbread and other confectionery. Today, it is not unusual to find a long queue waiting patiently to buy the gingerbread, still made to a secret recipe.

Take the A591 south
and east to **Rydal**.

→ • • • • • • • • • • • • **9**

9 RYDAL

There is little to the scattered grey-stone village of Rydal, strung out along the main road running north from Ambleside; but the nearby lake, **Rydal Water**, was a favourite spot of the Wordsworths, who would often picnic on its island. It lies sandwiched between the slopes of Nab Scar and Loughrigg Fell, and would often freeze over, providing the Wordsworth household with another opportunity for enjoyment – skating.

In the village, **Rydal Mount** was home to William Wordsworth and his family from 1813 to his death in 1850. He was at the peak of his fame at this time, though his best work had all been accomplished, mostly at Dove Cottage. The Wordsworth family continued to live at Rydal after his death, and his descendants still own and live in the house, which is open to the public during summer months and receives many visitors – as it did when Wordsworth lived there. The adjoining garden is still very much as Wordsworth – who had strong views on how a garden should look – designed it.

10 AMBLESIDE

Lying half a mile north of Lake Windermere, Ambleside is a large Lakeland village almost entirely composed of slate; even new development in the centre of the town maintains this tradition.

.The tiny and much photographed **Bridge House**, standing on what was probably an old packhorse bridge spanning Stock Ghyll, was immortalised by Turner and Ruskin, and is now an information centre. Built in the 18th century as a covered bridge and the summer house of the now demolished Ambleside Hall, it is said to have once housed a family with six children.

To the east of Ambleside lies Wansfell, an uphill but moderate walk that offers a truly fabulous view down the length of Lake Windermere and over the neigh-bouring valley of Troutbeck. Closer to town, in a wooded ravine, **Stockghyll Force**, an attractive waterfall and beck that for hundreds of years powered a wide range of mills, has been a popular stroll since Victorian times.

Clockwise from top left:
Dove Cottage, Grasmere;
the pier, Ambleside; Bridge
House, Ambleside; Rydal
Mount; Wordsworth
memorabilia and portrait,
Dove Cottage, Grasmere

Continue south on the
A591 for 2 miles to
Ambleside. ⑩

Head west out of the
village to reach the A593.
Follow this for half a mile,
and then branch left on
B5286 to reach Hawkshead. ⑪

Continue through
Hawkshead and take the
B5285 south east to reach
⑫ *Far* and *Near Sawrey*.

11 HAWKSHEAD

Set midway between Ambleside and Coniston at the northern tip of Esthwaite Water, Hawkshead is a timeless place. The village grew up at the junction of packhorse trails that were developed to link the early Windermere ferries with the Coniston valley. It was not until the 19th century that roads penetrated as far as the village, though today its centre, a snug arrangement of narrow cobbled streets and alleys leading to secluded courtyards, is banned to traffic.

Though born in Cockermouth *(see p20)*, Wordsworth attended the **grammar school** here (open to the public), and it is easy to see how the village and its setting would have inspired him in his earlier works. The **Beatrix Potter Gallery** contains a selection of original drawings by the artist, together with a display telling the story of her life. The building was once the office of her husband, solicitor William Heelis, and remains largely unaltered since his day.

To the south of Hawkshead, the landscape is dominated by the green mantle of **Grizedale Forest Park**. Walking and cycling are easy and popular here, with eight walking trails and five cycle trails to follow. The Ridding Wood Trail is surfaced throughout and passes 20 pieces of contemporary forest sculpture.

Clockwise from below:
view across Esthwaite Water;
boats on Lake Windermere;
Hill Top Farm, Sawrey

BEATRIX POTTER

Beatrix Potter (1866–1947) was brought up in London but her parents took her on a summer holiday to Ambleside when she was 16. She loved Derwent Water, and explored the Newlands valley and watched wildlife in the woods, and made many sketches of the landscape. When back in London, Beatrix started a book that eventually became *The Tale of Peter Rabbit*, published in 1902. It was an instant success, and she went on to write two books a year for the next 10 years. Beatrix purchased Hill Top Farm near Sawrey with the proceeds and eventually moved there in 1913. After her marriage she wrote less and less and became more involved in conservation of the Lake District countryside, and left some 800ha (4,000 acres) to the National Trust.

12 FAR SAWREY AND NEAR SAWREY

The two small villages of Far Sawrey and Near Sawrey lie between the lake of Windermere and **Esthwaite Water** amid a rolling, wooded landscape and on a lane that runs down to the Windermere ferry. Near Sawrey is renowned for its association with Beatrix Potter. The 17th-century **Hill Top** farm was acquired with royalties from her first book, *Peter Rabbit*, and it was here that she created the world of *Jemima Puddle-Duck* and *Pigling Bland*. When she died in 1947, Potter bequeathed Hill Top to the National Trust subject to the condition that is was kept exactly as she had left it.

13 LAKE WINDERMERE

Windermere is the largest lake in England (10 miles long and one mile wide at its broadest point), and its surrounds are among the most beautiful in the country. Much of the shoreline is wooded, islands punctuate its middle reaches and high ground flanks much of the lake, providing excellent vantage points.

The lake is renowned for char and deep-water trout, the former, in its potted form, being a considerable delicacy among the wealthy families of the 17th and 18th centuries. By the middle of the 19th century, however, as Victorian tourists came to explore the 'Lake Mountains', sailing for pleasure here became an important attraction, and so it has remained. **Bowness-on-Windermere** is a sprawling tourist town that developed after the arrival of the railway at Windermere town in 1847. Before then this was no more than a small group of cottages and huts used by fishermen. Today it is a bustling place, with lake boats constantly coming and going. Bowness also marks the end of the Dales Way, a middle-distance walk that begins in Ilkley. To its north, at a place where barges used to unload gravel dredged from the lake bed, the Windermere **Steamboat Museum** houses a unique collection of historic steamboats and motorboats, including the *Dolly*, reputedly the oldest mechanically powered boat in the world.

Continue east on the B5285 until you reach **Lake Windermere**. Take the ferry, and then turn left on the A592 to and then Windermere via Bowness-on-Windermere. **13**

From Windermere turn right on to the A591 to return to **Kendal**.

← • • • • • • • • • • • **1**

WITH MORE TIME

Muncaster Castle, set in beautiful gardens in Eskdale, west of Coniston Water, has been the home of the Pennington family since the 1200s. Open to the public, and said to be haunted, it contains a wide variety of historic furniture, some fine tapestries, and paintings by renowned artists such as Reynolds and Gainsborough.

To the south, the region of Furness (the hinterland of Barrow-in-Furness) owes most of its economic development to the exploitation of its natural resources by the monks of **Furness Abbey** *(left)*. The 12th-century abbey was and still is one of the most important monastic sites in the country.

Lancaster and the rural uplands of the Forest of Bowland

North Lancashire is a verdant region, though the legacy of its industrial past still lingers in more than a few corners. The tussocky moorlands and flower-filled river valleys of the Forest of Bowland surround stone villages and characterful towns. Two rivers influence the region's landscape: the Lune to the north and the Ribble to the south, which takes a picturesque route through Clitheroe.

TOUR ROUTE

Lancaster ①
Forest of Bowland ②
Chipping ③
Clitheroe ④
Austwick, Clapham and Ingleton ⑤
Kirkby Lonsdale ⑥
Arnside and Silverdale ⑦
Carnforth ⑧
Morecambe ⑨

TOUR LENGTH

DISTANCE approx. 105 miles (165km)
DURATION 3 days

TOURIST INFORMATION CENTRES

CLITHEROE 12–14 Market Place, BB7 2DA;
01200 425566
LANCASTER 29 Castle Hill LA1 1YN; 01524 32878
MORECAMBE Old Station Buildings, Marine Road Central LA4 4DB; 01524 582808

Clockwise from far left:
packhorse bridge at
Clapham; Littledale, Forest
of Bowland; statue of Eric
Morecambe, Morecambe;
view of Ashton
Memorial, Lancaster

1 LANCASTER

Essentially Georgian, the vibrant city of Lancaster sits on the banks of the River Lune. Its 12th-century **castle,** known as John of Gaunt's castle, was an important stronghold and is still one of Europe's longest-serving operational prisons. Among the many individuals brought to Lancaster for trial , the most famous were the Pendle Witches *(see p33)*. The Grand Jury Room includes some superb Gillow furniture *(see p34)*, while the branding iron used on prisoners can still be seen in the Crown Court. Visitors can even briefly experience what it is like to be locked in a dungeon. Rising above **Williamson Park**, the elegant **Ashton Memorial** dominates the city skyline. The memorial was commissioned by Lancastrian millionaire Lord Ashton, in memory of his wife. The park has plenty to offer including a tropical butterfly house and an exotic birds enclosure, as well as beautiful parkland walks.

Leave Lancaster south
on the A6, and on the
outskirts take unclassified
roads south east towards
Quernmore crossing the
Forest of Bowland before
descending through
Dunsop Bridge to reach
Slaidburn via the B6478. **2**

2 FOREST OF BOWLAND

An area of wild and windswept beauty, the Forest of Bowland is not a 'forest' as such, but a former hunting domain. This peaty, gritstone moorland landscape is networked by deep river valleys and where kings and nobles once hunted wild boar, deer and wolves. High on the moors, the road snakes through a pass known as the Trough of Bowland, a traditional packhorse way once used to convey the Pendle Witches to Lancaster for trial. The remote amber-stone village of **Slaidburn**, isolated and protected by the surrounding fells, and largely owned by the Fletcher family for almost 200 years, has remained virtually unchanged since the early 19th century. The church is distinctive for its unusual arrangement of Georgian box-pews, an 18th-century triple-decker pulpit, and exquisite carved screens.

Return to Dunsop Bridge
and follow unclassified
roads south through
Whitewell to **Chipping**.
3

⊕ *Leave Chipping on local roads signposted for **Clitheroe**, to reach the B6243 on the outskirts* ④ *of the town.*

3 CHIPPING

Chipping, with its lovely mellow stone buildings and narrow streets, is tucked away beneath the Bowland fells in the heart of the Ribble Valley. The village retains much of its 17th-century layout, especially along Windy Street. It is worth looking inside the **Church of St Bartholomew** for its amusing figureheads carved on a pillar in the north aisle. Chipping thrived during the Industrial Revolution when seven mills were located along Chipping Brook, although only a chairmaking factory survives today.

4 CLITHEROE

One of the oldest towns in Lancashire, Clitheroe is centred around its 12th-century **castle**. Standing on a rocky outcrop of limestone above the River Ribble, the keep, one of the smallest in England, is nevertheless a prominent landmark. It is the only remaining castle in Lancashire that had a Royalist garrison during the Civil War. There is a small museum of local history adjoining the keep. Clitheroe itself has a delightful, traditional feel about it. A market has been held here since 1283 and still takes place three times a week. To the south of town rises the brooding dome of **Pendle Hill**, famed for its association with witchcraft, but also where George Fox supposedly had a vision that inspired him to found the Quaker movement.

⊕ *Take the A671 east out of Clitheroe to reach the A59, and follow this to Gisburn, turning left onto the A682 to join the A65 at Long Preston. Follow the A65 north to **Ingleton** via* ⑤ ***Austwick** and **Clapham**.*

*On leaving Ingleton, turn right on to the A65, and follow this for 6 miles to **Kirkby Lonsdale**.*

→ • • • • • • • • • • ⑥

5 AUSTWICK, CLAPHAM AND INGLETON

On the edge of limestone country, **Austwick** draws walkers who come to explore the surrounding countryside and the **Norber Erratics**. Deposited around 11,000 years ago by a retreating glacier, this group of boulders are a local geological curiosity. Set in beautiful Dales scenery featuring waterfalls and stands of ancient trees, nearby **Clapham** is a delight with its old stone houses and bridges. Within reach of the village are gorges and Britain's largest cavern, **Gaping Gill**, into which tumbles Britain's highest unbroken waterfall. It takes its name from its vast entrance, which swallows the waters of Fell Beck as they gather from the high grounds around Ingleborough. The main chamber is an incredible 140m (460ft) long and almost 30m (100ft) high and wide. **Ingleborough Cave**, also easily reached from Clapham through Clapdale Woods, is similarly spectacular with its impressive, 350-million-year-old stalactites and stalagmites, all atmospherically floodlit. The next village, Ingleton, capitalises on its limestone setting too: the underground world of **White Scar Caves** is Britain's longest show cave. The easy walk through woodland gorges at the edge of the village is spectacular all year round.

Clockwise from top left:
John Ruskin's view from Kirkby Lonsdale; Clapham; Devil's Bridge, Kirkby Londsdale; Clitheroe Castle

THE LANCASHIRE WITCHES

One of the most famous events to take place in Lancashire occurred during the 17th century, and has since formed the basis of novels, and radio and television programmes. With the ascension of James I to the English throne in 1603, there came a new wave of persecution for those who were involved with witchcraft, such as the 13 so-called Pendle Witches, who were tried and hanged at Lancaster Castle in 1612. Two families were at the centre of the Pendle case. Significantly, both were headed by elderly widows who were known locally by their nicknames: Old Demdike and Old Chattox.

6 KIRKBY LONSDALE

The lovely and historic market town of Kirkby Lonsdale is set in an area of great natural beauty. From the medieval Devil's Bridge you can admire the views that so inspired John Ruskin and were painted by J W Turner, or simply get an excellent bacon 'buttie' and mug of tea from the bridge cafe. Don't be suprised to find hordes of amiable bikers congregating at the bridge on sunny weekends: over the years they have become a cult tourist attraction in themselves.

*From Kirkby Lonsdale return to the A65 heading north west for 5 miles to the junction with the A6070. Take the first left onto the A6070 for 1 mile, and then take local roads west cross country to **Arnside** and **Silverdale**.*

⊕ Leave Silverdale east by
• following signs for Yealand
• Redmayne, and in the
• village turn onto the
• A6 south and follow the
8 road to *Carnforth*.

7 ARNSIDE AND SILVERDALE

Located in an Area of Outstanding Natural Beauty, the seaside town of **Arnside** looks out across the Kent Estuary and the hills of the southern Lake District beyond. From the wooded hill of Arnside Knott and the neighbouring village of **Silverdale** to the south, there are unrivalled views of the vast spread of Morecambe Bay. There are lovely walks out of Silverdale to the headland of Jack Scout, owned mostly by the National Trust.

Nearby, **Leighton Moss Nature Reserve** is a vast and popular nature reserve with some rare species of breeding birds among the many thousands that flock to its wetlands. Above the reserve stands the stately neogothic **Leighton Hall**, owned and lived in by the descendents of the furniture-making Gillow dynasty as it has been for centuries. Consequently, the house has all the atmosphere of a family home, and visitors are invited to sit on the ancient chairs while knowledgeable guides reveal the hall's history. You are even welcome to take your place at the 18th-century dining table or to play a tune on the Steinway! As well as landscaped parkland and woodland walks, Leighton has a pretty 19th-century walled garden – the passion of the present owner – featuring rose-covered walls, a fragrant herb patch and an overflowing herbaceous border.

Take the A6 south through
Bolton-le-Sands, eventually
branching right onto the
A5105 for 3 miles to reach
Morecambe.

→ • • • • • • • • • • • **9**

8 CARNFORTH

This small Victorian market town is always busy and gains all the breezy benefits of its location on the edge of Morecambe Bay. But its fame rests on the fact that in 1945 *Brief Encounter*, starring Celia Johnson and Trevor Howard, was filmed in Carnforth **station**. The film is a love story about a man and a woman, both married but not to each other, who meet in the refreshment room at a railway station. Carnforth station cafe is now a nostalgic spot for film buffs. The town also offers some nice walks along the River Keer, the bay and the Lancaster Canal.

THE GILLOWS OF LEIGHTON HALL

The Lancaster branch of the Gillows family has been making furniture as well as architectural joinery and billiard tables, encouraged by the game's vogue, since the 1770s. The Gillows were shrewd in producing a neat, rather conventional range of furniture derived from the designs of James Wyatt, the most fashionable architect of the last two decades of the 18th century, and from plates in the pattern-books of George Hepplewhite and Thomas Sheraton. They avoided the height of fashion, supplying instead pieces that would appeal to the burgeoning middle classes of Liverpool and Manchester, who valued good, solid, well-made furniture.

Clockwise from top right:
Morecambe Bay;
Leighton Hall

9 MORECAMBE

In the early 19th century, Morecambe was simply a small fishing village called Poulton-le-Sands, but it blossomed into one of the most attractive and popular holiday resorts in Lancashire. For years, there was a sense of rivalry with Blackpool, as Morecambe always had a lively character and style, one highlighted by the zany half of a famous comedy duo Morecambe and Wise. There is a lovely statue of locally born Eric Morecambe on the promenade. Another native, actress Dame Thora Hird, made her stage debut in 1911 at the age of two months when she was carried on stage at Morecambe's Royalty Theatre in a play directed by her father. The huge expanse of Morecambe Bay once offered the shortest route into Furness, or Lancashire-over-the-Sands as it was previously known. You need the company of a guide to cross safely today *(see p24)*, but the experience is unforgettable: vast skies, a seemingly limitless sprawl of sand and river, and an awesome sense of place.

*Leave Morecambe by following the B5274 east to the A589 and then take the A6 to return to **Lancaster**.*

WITH MORE TIME

Bright, brash and breezy is the only way to describe **Blackpool** *(left)*. A long-established holiday resort that formerly served the mill workers of Lancashire, the town now draws crowds from across Britain – anyone, really, who just wants to let their hair down for a few fun-filled days. In contrast, a short way south along the coast is **Lytham** – and **St Anne's** – two small genteel towns traditionally joined as one. Here you can enjoy the fine promenade, peaceful parks, beautiful gardens and admire the town's old half-timbered buildings.

The unexpected attractions of Lancashire's coastal plain

The flat expanse of the Lancashire coastal plain was created by draining once-inaccessible marshland, and most of this region is now farming country. The remaining fen-meadows are renowned for the large numbers of birds that roost here during the winter months. Along the dune-fringed coast lies the typical, fun-oriented seaside resort of Southport, which contrasts with workaday inland towns like Wigan and Preston.

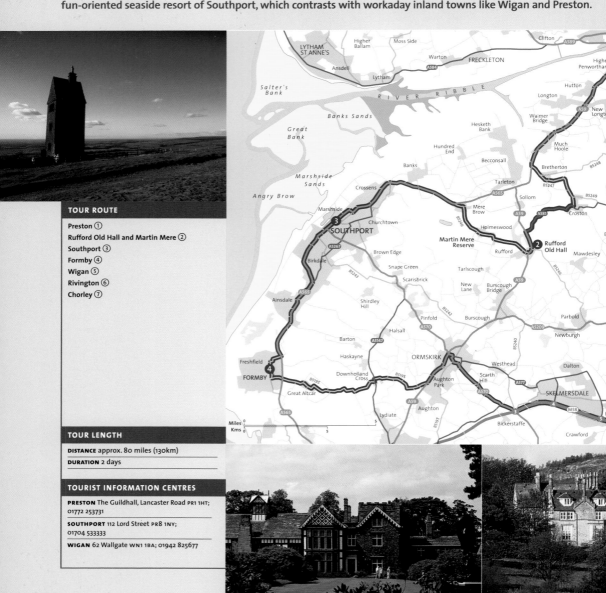

TOUR ROUTE

Preston ①
Rufford Old Hall and Martin Mere ②
Southport ③
Formby ④
Wigan ⑤
Rivington ⑥
Chorley ⑦

TOUR LENGTH

DISTANCE approx. 80 miles (130km)

DURATION 2 days

TOURIST INFORMATION CENTRES

PRESTON The Guildhall, Lancaster Road PR1 1HT; 01772 253731

SOUTHPORT 112 Lord Street PR8 1NY; 01704 533333

WIGAN 62 Wallgate WN1 1BA; 01942 825677

Clockwise from far left:
Rivington Moor; riding on
the beach near Southport;
Rivington reservoirs;
Rufford Old Hall

1 PRESTON

Granted city status as recently as 2002, Preston is a
dynamic regional capital but one that still nurtures its
splendid old buildings, like the 1893 **Harris Museum and
Art Gallery**, one of the first Greek revival buildings in
Britain. Today, it holds a wide-ranging collection of art
and hosts regular exhibitions, which often explore the
city's Asian heritage. In the city centre, the tiny Georgian
oasis of **Winckley Square** is where Preston's wealthiest
merchant's used to live, and close by is the expansive
Avenham Park, whose wooded slopes lead down to the
River Ribble. The city dates from the 7th century, but in
1179 this medieval market town received an important
charter giving Preston the right to hold a 'Guild Merchant'
every 20 years: the next meeting is in 2012, and it
demonstrates the influence held by local traders. The
city's football team – Preston North End FC – were
founder members of the Football League, and the home
ground of Deepdale is where you'll find the **National
Football Museum**, arguably the finest collection of
football memorabilia in Britain.

2 RUFFORD OLD HALL AND MARTIN MERE

Home to the Hesketh family for 400 years, **Rufford Old
Hall** is one of the finest buildings in Lancashire, with its
impressive timber-framed Tudor hall. By the middle of
the 18th century, manor houses such as this were
considered unsuited to domestic life, and the family
moved to Rufford New Hall, a more comfortable mansion
half a mile away. The spectacular Great Hall has an
intricately carved 'moveable' wooden screen and a
dramatic hammer-beam roof, and the house contains
fine collections of 16th- and 17th-century oak furniture,
arms, armour and tapestries. The grounds are laid out
in late-Victorian style and feature a herbaceous border,
orchard, topiary, sculptures and a woodland walk.

En route to Southport, it is worth stopping at the
Martin Mere, a wildlife reserve where visitors can get
really close to some exotic species of birds, as well as
more familiar ones. The surrounding marshlands – the
mere – are an important wintering ground for swans
and geese, as well as some rarer species.

*Leave Preston south west
on the A59 and after 7
miles branch left onto the
B5247 down to Croston.
From here, take the A581
west to rejoin the A59 and
turn left for Rufford Old
Hall. From Rufford take the
B5246 west towards
Southport and follow signs
to Martin Mere.* ❷

*Take the B5246 west to join
the A565 to Marshside and
on to Southport.*

 ❸

Follow the A565
south along the
4 coast to *Formby*.

3 SOUTHPORT

The coastal flats of **Marshside** to the north of
Southport have some of the best wet grassland in the
north west of England. This area along the Ribble
Estuary is recognised as one of Britain's premier
birdwatching locations, and to date some 300 bird
species have been recorded here. Southport,
by contrast, is a bustling seaside town: mile-long Lord
Street is the main thoroughfare, with its attractive
Georgian and Victorian buildings often bright with
floral displays in summer. On the coast there's
Pleasureland, the 'entertainment' zone, full of the
excitement and thrills associated with a seaside fun
park. Southport beach is expansive and one from which
you can admire the recently restored Southport pier.

4 FORMBY

The coast around Formby is the largest area of
undeveloped dunes and coastal woodland in England,
and home to rare species like the natterjack toad and
sand lizard. These windswept inter-tidal flats, which
extend from Southport to the Mersey Estuary, are
renowned for their Neolithic human footprints and
those of animals that grazed the salt marshes in this
period. The small and unremarkable town of Formby
has been cut off from the sea by the shifting sands of
Formby Point, now a two-mile stretch of dunes with
extensive views across Crosby Channel and Liverpool
Bay to the distant hills of north Wales. The nearby
Formby Point Squirrel Reserve is one of the best places
in England to see the red squirrel. Elsewhere they have
declined due to disease and competition from grey
squirrels, but here you can get up close, and even get
them to eat from your hand.

Take the B5195 to reach the
A59. Turn left into Ormskirk,
and then take the A570
and follow this south to
join the M58. Follow the
motorway east until you
reach the M6. Go under the
motorway, onto a slip road
to Orrell then take the A577
5 east into *Wigan*.

Clockwise from above:
Wigan Pier museum;
Southport pier;
Astley Hall

5 WIGAN

Once the butt of music hall jokes and the unflattering
subject of George Orwell's *The Road to Wigan Pier*,
modern Wigan is an energetic town with a toe in
Greater Manchester but its heart very much in
Lancashire. It has a passion for football and rugby
league, but has become popular for the imaginative
development at **Wigan Pier**, on the Leeds and Liverpool
Canal. The key attraction is here is The Way We Were, an
authentic recreation of life in the 1900s in Wigan and
surrounding Lancashire.

LANCASHIRE CHEESES

General de Gaulle complained about the
difficulty of governing a nation with 246
varieties of cheese; British prime ministers
have an even more daunting task – Britain has
over 450 specialist cheeses, and ten of them
(plus a whole range of variants) come from
Lancashire: Butlers Trotter Hill Tasty, Dew-Lay
Creamy, Garstang Blue, Crumbly, Garlic,
Lancashire with Black Pepper, Smoked,
Lancashire Black Bombs, award-winning Mrs
Kirkham's, and Sykes Fell. With the possible
exception of Mrs Kirkham's, these cheeses
are found only in Lancashire.

Take the B5238 north east
via Aspull, turn left and
then right onto the B6226
for Horwich then left into
Lever Park. Follow the
unclassified road through
Lever Park to *Rivington*.

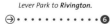 6

6 RIVINGTON

The wooded area around the village of Rivington is one of the most popular walking and cycling areas in south Lancashire. The focal point is the man-made reservoirs, extending northwards to Anglezarke, now a magnet for local birdwatchers. There are two contrasting landscapes around Rivington: one is the wooded remains of industrialist Lord Leverhulme's estate, which led to the creation of the gardens at **Lever Park**; the other is the wild, windswept uplands of the **West Pennine Moors**, a vast area that extends eastwards to Rossendale. An easily visible landmark is the modest hump of **Rivington Pike** perched on the flank of Winter Hill; there are splendid views from here reaching as far as the mountains of north Wales.

7 CHORLEY

The birthplace of Henry Tate, the sugar magnate and founder of the Tate Gallery, Chorley has a modern, buzzing centre that revolves around its traditional market. On the edge of town is Astley Park, a huge area of invigorating parkland surrounding the fine Elizabethan **Astley Hall**, with its beautiful if not quite symmetrical façade of mullioned windows set in red brick. Today, the hall houses changing displays and collections, and stages interactive events. The nearby theme park of **Camelot** at Charnock Richard, with its emphasis on King Arthur and the Knights of the Round Table, is hugely popular. For those interested in more tangeable history, the complex holds an extensive indoor antiques and collectables market each Sunday, as well as regular antiques auctions.

*Continue on local roads north to **Chorley**. Camelot is a few miles west of Chorley.*

*Leave Chorley on the ring road to the A6. Turn right to join the M61 (northbound). Turn left onto the M65, and follow this to its end and then take the dual carriageway north back to **Preston**.*

WITH MORE TIME

The Isle of Man (*left*) – seat of the world's longest continuous parliament, the Tynwald – is still as popular a destination with Lancashire folk as it was in the days when mining and mill families would take their holidays there. The island, accessible by air from Liverpool, Manchester and Blackpool, and by sea from Heysham and Liverpool, is renowned for its scenery. In addition to its famous TT motorbike races, the Isle of Man now holds an annual walking festival to which the island is perfectly suited.

West Yorkshire's Brontë country

If you haven't tasted one of Betty's Fat Rascals, you haven't lived. Some might add Harry Ramsden's legendary fish and chips from Guiseley to a list of quintessential other Yorkshire experiences. For these and many other reasons, the slice of God's own country between Harrogate and Hebden Bridge is a tasty morsel. A varied menu includes the delights of the Brontë Parsonage Museum, Saltaire's industrial heritage and modern art, and the steam railway at Keighley – and the wide open moorlands at Haworth to work off all those calories.

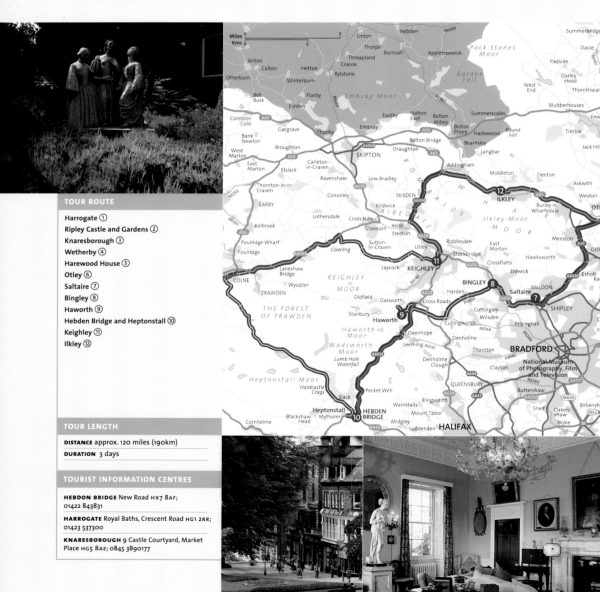

TOUR ROUTE

Harrogate ①
Ripley Castle and Gardens ②
Knaresborough ③
Wetherby ④
Harewood House ⑤
Otley ⑥
Saltaire ⑦
Bingley ⑧
Haworth ⑨
Hebden Bridge and Heptonstall ⑩
Keighley ⑪
Ilkley ⑫

TOUR LENGTH

DISTANCE approx. 120 miles (190km)

DURATION 3 days

TOURIST INFORMATION CENTRES

HEBDON BRIDGE New Road HX7 8AF;
01422 843831

HARROGATE Royal Baths, Crescent Road HG1 2RR;
01423 537300

KNARESBOROUGH 9 Castle Courtyard, Market
Place HG5 8AE; 0845 3890177

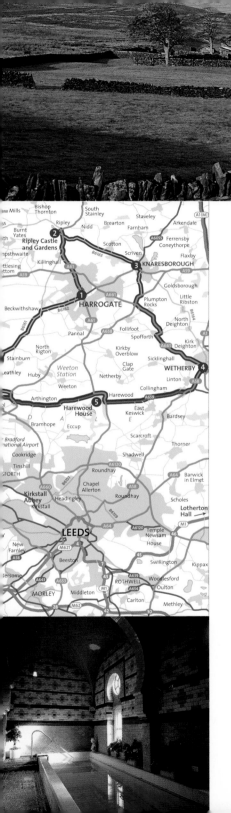

Clockwise from far left:
Brontë Parsonage Museum;
countryside round Haworth;
Turkish Baths, Harrogate;
drawing room, Ripley
Castle; Harrogate

1 HARROGATE

Harrogate is the archetypal English spa town, famed for its medicinal springs, public gardens and fine architecture. These days, revenue from hydropathic health cures has been largely replaced by a busy round of conferences, exhibitions and trade fairs hosted in the modern Harrogate International Centre. But many pleasing buildings survive from Harrogate's heyday in the late 19th century, notably its grand hotels. The sulphurous waters still run free of charge at the **Royal Pump Rooms Art Gallery and Museum** (1842), and still taste vile enough to do you a power of good. But the wells are enclosed by glass screens to reduce the typically sulphurous 'rotten eggs' smell. More modern, appealing water therapies are offered in the shape of a health and beauty spa in the extensively restored and exotically tiled late-19th-century **Turkish Baths**. The **Mercer Art Gallery** makes use of an early spa building too. A large stretch of open parkland called **The Stray** sweeps through the centre of town, while spring bulbs and formal beds brighten the typically Victorian **Valley Gardens**, where there is a boating lake, a teahouse and a bandstand. On the south western outskirts of town, the superb **Harlow Carr Gardens** are the Royal Horticultural Society's northern pride and joy – the Streamside Garden is a magnificent sight all summer long. The surrounding moors seem to encroach on the garden with a blaze of heather when not much else is flowering. You can stop for afternoon tea in one of **Betty's Cafe Tea Rooms** renowned teashops here as well as in town. The orginal Betty's was started in Harrogate by a Swiss confectioner in 1907 and has become a highly successful 'micro-chain' of Yorkshire teashops. Betty's still operates as a family firm, deliberately kept small so that every detail, down to the exact blend of tea, is monitored.

From Harrogate take the A61 north for 3 miles to **Ripley Castle and Gardens**.

Clockwise from above:
viaduct at Knaresborough;
Harewood House; Bramham
Park, Wetherby;
Knaresborough Castle

Head south east
on the B6165 to
③ Knaresborough.

Head south to the A661
and then turn left
④ towards Wetherby.

Head south from Wetherby
on the A58, and join the
A659 west following signs
to Harewood House.
→ · · · · · · · · · · · · · ⑤

2 RIPLEY CASTLE AND GARDENS

Ripley Castle, set on the banks of the River Nidd, has been the home of the Ingilby family for nearly 700 years. The interior is noted for its fine paintings, furnishings, chandeliers and portraits, including one of Sir John Ingilby holding plans of the house. The most notable room is the library in the Tudor keep, where 'Trooper' Jane Ingilby supposedly held Oliver Cromwell at gunpoint. However, the Knight's Chamber is by far the most spectacular with its 16th-century oak ceiling, a priest's hiding hole, and its superb collection of arms and armour from the English Civil War. The castle terrace offers fantastic views over the magnificent gardens and the lakes beyond. You can follow a park walk round the ornamental lake and into the deer park itself. It is also worth taking a peek at the walled kitchen garden with its extensive herb bed and an extraordinary collection of rare vegetables. The quaint village of Ripley was built by Sir William Amscotts Ingilby in the 1820s and is modelled on a village in Alsace-Lorraine that he so admired.

3 KNARESBOROUGH

Perched on the craggy lip of the Nidd Gorge, Knaresborough enjoys one of the most striking settings in North Yorkshire. Amid its ample stock of well-kept period houses (many of them Georgian) crammed into a maze of intricate alleys, there's a lot to see. Notice the curious troglodytic folly known as the House in the Rock, and the wonderful chemist's shop on the Market Square (the oldest in England, dating from 1720), which makes its own lavender water. There's an ancient castle, a medieval hermitage, and a railway viaduct bestriding the deep gorge. Knaresborough's colourful characters also play a part in the tourism industry. Besides the red-coated town crier keeping visitors up with the news on market day, there's no avoiding Old Mother Shipton, a 16th-century soothsayer who narrowly escaped being burnt as a witch for her uncannily accurate predictions. Her spooky riverside cave dwelling pulls in the crowds, along with a petrifying well whose mineral-rich waters turn anything placed in them to 'stone' within weeks.

4 WETHERBY

The north western approach road to Wetherby takes you past the picturesque ruins of Spofforth Castle, cunningly shoehorned into a rocky, naturally defensive site. Stockeld Park, one mile nearer the town, is a fine 18th-century house with an extra-wide staircase designed to accommodate the broad-beamed crinoline ballgowns of the time. Wetherby itself is an agreeable former coaching stop on the Great North Road with a well-preserved legacy of period buildings and traditional speciality shops. It holds regular produce and farmers' markets, and is well known among followers of form as a steeplechasing venue. Bramham Park, on the southern side of the town, is a mini-Versailles with its formal cascades, lakes and temples. The handsome Queen Anne mansion was damaged by fire in 1828, but its ornate Baroque interior still displays a fine show of French furnishings and sporting pictures.

5 HAREWOOD HOUSE

The seat of the earls of Harewood was built in 1759 by John Carr. Clearly, no expense was spared to make this grand house outshine its local rivals, though the original design was modified in the 19th and 20th centuries. 'Capability' Brown landscaping deploys a cascade and wooded grounds, brilliant with rhododendrons and bog garden plants in early summer, that sweep down to a lake. Inside, Adam plasterwork and Chippendale furniture enhance outstanding collections of watercolours and porcelain. The restored state bed stands ready for any royal visitation. Modern art and a 'below stairs' exhibition add a welcome change of pace.

6 OTLEY

Thomas Chippendale's Wharfedale birthplace is a handsome little town, one of its attractions being that the pubs stay open all day long on Fridays (market day). Rumour has it that Cromwell's Ironsides drank the Black Bull inn dry on their way to the Battle of Marston Moor in 1644, yet still managed to win a decisive victory. Otley's older vernacular buildings are a well-kept mix of mainly Georgian and Victorian styles, making the town a suitable stand-in for Emmerdale's fictional Hotton. The four-faced Jubilee clock is a useful, if chimeless, timekeeper on the main street, while **Chevin Forest Park** on Otley's south eastern outskirts is a scenic place for a stroll. En route to Saltaire stop off at Guiseley for some of **Harry Ramsden's** famous fish and chips at the White Cross roundabout.

7 SALTAIRE

Now a World Heritage Site, this model factory township attracts many permanent residents as well as transient visitors. When the worker's cottages were first built here, Saltaire enjoyed a distinctly more rural outlook than it does today. It was developed in the mid-19th century by Titus Salt, an enterprising textile tycoon whose penchant for the Italian Renaissance gave his mill complex an unexpectedly Mediterranean appearance. Look for the llamas (alpacas) on Saltaire's ubiquitous coat of arms – those silky coats provided the cash for this ambitious project. The former mill, in the style of a Tuscan palazzo, once housed over a thousand clattering looms, today replaced by an upmarket shopping centre and the **1853 Gallery**, Europe's largest permanent collection of the works of Bradford-born artist David Hockney. The **Victorian Reed Organ and Harmonium Museum** has some eye-catching exhibits, and a few may bend your ear too.

Continue west along the A659 as far as Otley. 6

Take the A65 and A6038 south to Shipley; turn right on the A650, following signs for Saltaire. 7

Continue north west on the A650 to Bingley.

8

Clockwise from above view near Haworth; Five Rise Locks, Bingley; Ilkley Moor

8 BINGLEY

Bingley's main claim to fame is a prodigious flight of locks on the Leeds and Liverpool Canal. **Five Rise Locks** presents a logistical challenge even to experienced boat-handlers, shifting some 18m (60ft) in height in just five ingeniously interconnected stages. It is impossible to empty any of the locks unless the one below it is also empty. The canal was built between 1770 and 1816, encouraged by a consortium of Bradford businessmen anxious to transport goods to Liverpool. Until 2001 it remained the sole waterway to cross the Pennines.

Take the B6429 to Cullingworth, then turn right on the B6144 following signs to
9 *Haworth.*

9 HAWORTH

Brontë fans know that this bleak moorland village was the home of the famous literary sisters whose cruelly curtailed lives and enduringly popular novels have made it a place of pilgrimage. The Georgian parsonage that is now the **Brontë Parsonage Museum** lies beyond the craft and antique shops on the cobbled main street. Here you can see the table where those tales of repressed passion were penned, and the horsehair sofa where Emily died. Other destinations on the Brontë trail are the Sunday school where the sisters taught, the family vault in the parish church, and the Black Bull inn where brother Branwell drank himself into insensibility. After the museum, you can head up the path past the Brontë waterfalls to **Top Withens**, the roofless ruin overlooking a panorama of windswept moorland that many allege was the inspiration for *Wuthering Heights*.

Take the A6033 south as far as **Hebden Bridge** *and* **Heptonstall**.

10

THE BRONTË SISTERS

Irish-born Patrick Brunty changed his name to the more distinguished-sounding Brontë as he moved up in the world following his ordination into the church. He moved to Haworth in 1820 with his Cornish wife Maria and their two eldest children, who died soon afterwards. Their surviving four children remained at home, the girls creating imaginary worlds from books, while their brother Branwell fell gradually into debt and disgrace under the influence of opium and alcohol. The novels *Jane Eyre* (Charlotte), *Wuthering Heights* (Emily) and *Agnes Grey* (Anne) were the result – all published in 1847, catapulting the reclusive sisters into fame. Sadly, Branwell, Emily and Anne soon succumbed to the tuberculosis induced by their damp and draughty surroundings at Haworth, but Charlotte survived to marry, although she too died within a year. True classics, the greatest Brontë novels are still read avidly today.

10 HEBDEN BRIDGE AND HEPTONSTALL

These miniature Victorian mill towns virtually merge above Calderdale. Down in the valley, Hebden Bridge was originally a packhorse stop on the Rochdale canal. Textiles brought prosperity in the 19th century, but since the 1960s it has become a sort of Yorkshire Hampstead, a haunt of artists and intellectuals seeking alternative lifestyles. Perched on steep terraces to the west, the older weaving community of Heptonstall is a handsome little place and claims the world's oldest Methodist chapel in continual use. The hexagonal building dates from 1764, when John Wesley visited the village. The poet Sylvia Plath is buried in the local churchyard. From Hebden Bridge you can gain access to the Mary Towneley Loop, a circular national trail that forms part of the Pennine Bridleway. Another enjoyable walk leads up the valley to **Hardcastle Crags**, a wild beauty spot of tumbling water and fern-filled woodland now managed by the National Trust. **Gibson Mill**, at the heart of the property, has recently been restored as a flagship environmental project and exhibition centre.

11 KEIGHLEY

'Keethly', as it's pronounced, is a solid, much-expanded Victorian town with pleasantly old-fashioned shops in Cavendish Street. Its main visitor attraction is the steam-powered **Keighley and Worth Valley Railway**, which makes a memorably nostalgic way of reaching Haworth, and has starred in many period films requiring a steam train setting (notably *The Railway Children*). **Cliffe Castle Museum** has a local history exhibition housed in the lavish mansion of a wealthy textile magnate. To the north east of town, **East Riddlesden Hall** is a mullioned manor dating from 1648, full of splendid plasterwork and panelling, but imbued with dark legends relating to the Murgatroyds who once lived here.

12 ILKLEY

The very mention of this place is almost certain to get that relentless Yorkshire ditty churning through your head; the tourist authorities even package Ilkley as *Baht' at* Country. If this evokes an image of cloth caps and whippets, you've been misled; Ilkley is a decidedly superior little town of literary festivals and smart teashops. It has plenty of history too, much of it related in the **Manor House Museum and Art Gallery**, a 16th-century building near the church (where there are three Saxon crosses). The Romans established a garrison called Olicana here, but Ilkley really came into its own right as a Georgian spa town. The luxury hydros that profited from its icy moorland springs left a core of Victorian and Edwardian architecture and some handsome villas behind. Ilkley's famous moors swell to a crescendo on both sides of the town. Mysterious 'cup and ring' markings and a 'Swastika Stone' found here date from the Bronze Age.

 Take the minor road past Hardcastle Crags, over the exhilarating upland scenery of Heptonstall Moor, towards Colne. Turn right on to the A6068 towards Cowling, right again on minor roads, following signs for **Keighley**. ⑪

 Follow the A629 north up Airedale, turning right on the A6034 to Addingham, then right again on the A65 to **Ilkley**. ⑫

Take the A65 east to Otley, and follow signs to **Harrogate** via the A659, B6161 and B6162.

 ①

WITH MORE TIME

On the eastern side of Leeds you'll find **Lotherton Hall**, near Saxton, an Edwardian house with fascinating contents and fine grounds. Leeds and Bradford are full of interest, and you don't have to stray far into the urban jungle to find **Kirkstall Abbey** *(left)*, one of Britain's best-preserved Cistercian monasteries, with the Abbey House Museum of recreated Victoriana in its gatehouse. Bradford's star sight is the splendid **National Museum of Photography, Film and Television** with interactive galleries on the many ways of image-making.

The natural wonders of the southern Dales

On the south side of the Yorkshire Dales National Park, the Dales run mostly north to south, and road connections between valleys are sparse. But where your car cannot venture, hiking trails can often bridge the gaps across emerald-and-silver mosaics of whaleback hills, crystal waters and bare limestone. Sculpted over millennia, these tantalising glacial landscapes promise much more than a geology fieldtrip.

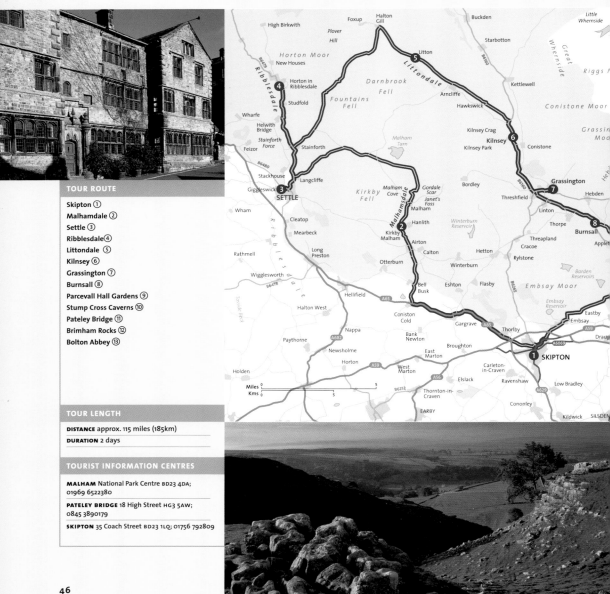

TOUR ROUTE

Skipton ①
Malhamdale ②
Settle ③
Ribblesdale ④
Littondale ⑤
Kilnsey ⑥
Grassington ⑦
Burnsall ⑧
Parcevall Hall Gardens ⑨
Stump Cross Caverns ⑩
Pateley Bridge ⑪
Brimham Rocks ⑫
Bolton Abbey ⑬

TOUR LENGTH

DISTANCE approx. 115 miles (185km)

DURATION 2 days

TOURIST INFORMATION CENTRES

MALHAM National Park Centre BD23 4DA; 01969 6522380

PATELEY BRIDGE 18 High Street HG3 5AW; 0845 3890179

SKIPTON 35 Coach Street BD23 1LQ; 01756 792809

1 SKIPTON

All major routes to the southern Dales pass through Skipton, which makes it a popular touring base, even though it is located just outside the national park. The town centre, a mix of ancient inns, 18th-century houses and modern shops, swings into action four times a week with one of the best markets in the area (the biggest is on Saturday). The converted old High Corn Mill and the glass-roofed Craven Court with its Victorian-style ironwork are two of the town's attractive shopping complexes. Skipton means 'sheeptown' but it is still an important cattle-auction centre too, retaining the odd set of traffic lights specifically dedicated to the safe passage of livestock. In the middle of town, the Norman **castle**, bearing the royalist Clifford family's resolute motto 'Desormais' ('Henceforth'), is remarkably intact given it survived a three-year Roundhead siege. After the Civil War Cromwell gave permission for the roof to be replaced as long as it was not strong enough to withstand the weight of a cannon. Inside, spot the quaint medieval loo cantilevered over the moat, and the exquisitely mullioned Conduit Court added in Henry VIII's reign. The town's **Holy Trinity Church** contains Clifford family tombs and an ornate 16th-century chancel screen. For a rundown on local history and much else besides, visit the **Craven Museum** in the old town hall. Among its multifarious exhibits is a small display commemorating Thomas Spencer, a Skipton lad who teamed up with Mr Marks to found a vast retailing empire.

*Leave Skipton on A65, heading westwards out of town as far as Coniston Cold, then turn right up towards Kirkby Malham and **Malhamdale**.*

Horton-in-Ribblesdale is renowned among hill-walkers for the Three Peaks Challenge, a punishing race held in April up the three landmark summits of Ribblehead: Pen-y-Ghent, Ingleborough and Whernside are all around 700m high (well over 2,000ft). The fastest competitors can scale the lot in under three hours. Less masochistic hikers can tackle this gruelling 23-mile route at a more leisurely pace at any time of year; but even so, you need to be very fit and experienced. Many find that just one peak will amply suffice for a day's march, but if you can manage all of them in a single day, you can join the Three Peaks of Yorkshire Club. The official starting point for the Three Peaks ascent is the Pen-y-Ghent cafe. Log in here, and they'll send out a search party if you aren't back by nightfall.

2 MALHAMDALE

So well tramped is the area around the headwaters of the River Aire that this dale on the Pennine Way is generally named after its main village, rather than Airedale as one might expect. **Kirkby Malham**, near the entrance to Malhamdale, has a notable church – St Michael's – with fine box pews and 16th-century roof timbers. Malham's helpful information centre points many visitors in the direction of the spectacular limestone features further up the valley. The Malham Trail takes in **Malham Cove**, a crescent wall of rock rearing 90m (290ft) above a natural amphitheatre. Formed on a geological fault-line, it has all the drama of an outdoor IMAX cinema screen. At the end of the ice age, cascades higher than Niagara Falls plummeted over its brim; today, the more modest Malham Beck runs underground, emerging from sinkholes at the base of the cliff. Blackened lichen and moss etch frown-lines on the pale stone, and all around you can see where frost and acidic meltwater have carved deep fissures or 'grikes' into the flat, bare rock. This limestone pavement is a rare habitat for harts-tongue ferns, orchids and dog's mercury. **Malham Tarn** to the north is Yorkshire's second-largest natural lake, another haunt of unusual birds and plantlife. While most water hereabouts swiftly disappears into the porous limestone, this sedgy tarn rests on a bed of slate covered with impervious glacial drift. **Gordale Scar**, the subject of a famous Turner painting, is a dramatic rock cleft where a stream leaps beneath overhanging crags. The smaller waterfall of Janet's Foss spills over a mossy tufa screen into a pool once used for dipping sheep.

Continue westwards on unclassified roads past Malham Tarn, following signs for **Settle**.

3 SETTLE

Like Skipton, Settle has a large and lively **market**, held here on Tuesdays. The town hall and arcaded Shambles (the old slaughterhouse) occupy centre-stage on the main square; steep lanes and sloping yards ripple off it in all directions past 17th-century terraces with dated door-cases, and upmarket shops full of walking boots, antique silver and second-hand books. The **Watershed Mill** is a former cotton mill-turned-visitor centre selling Dales products. The Folly on School Hill in the town centre is Settle's grandest house, built for a well-to-do tanner in 1675. The town is renowned as the starting point for one of Britain's most scenic rail routes, the **Settle-to-Carlisle Railway**. This ambitious Victorian engineering project (opened in 1876) carves 72 miles through Ribblesdale over wild moorland to the bucolic Eden Valley.

The unassuming town of **Giggleswick** on the opposite bank of the Ribble seems almost a suburb of Settle on a map. Period houses line the shady streets around the market cross and its public school, topped with a dome of green copper, dates from 1512. The birds of prey at the **Yorkshire Dales Falconry and Conservation Centre** show off their skills at regularly held shows.

4 RIBBLESDALE

A fine riverside walk leads along the Ribble Way from Langcliffe on the northern outskirts of Settle to **Stainforth**, a pretty village with a 17th-century pack-horse bridge and two waterfalls – **Stainforth Force** and **Catrigg Force**. Further up the valley, **Horton-in-Ribblesdale** dates back to Norman times. It is a straggling moorland village scarred in places by quarry workings. At the top of the valley, the scenery is austerely craggy, scattered with glacial drumlins and riddled with potholes. The **Ribblehead Viaduct**, built to carry the Settle-to-Carlisle Railway over a boggy stretch of Blea Moor, makes an unforgettable statement amid bleak surroundings. It strides across 24 arches rising 50m (165ft) above the valley floor, before disappearing into a long tunnel.

5 LITTONDALE

The unspoilt valley of Littondale takes its name from one of five villages on the River Skirfare, one of the River Wharfe's main tributaries. This is a haunt of keen walkers and nature lovers. If the light slants in a certain way along the valley sides, you may notice the pattern of ancient terraces known as lynchets, remnants of a medieval strip-farming system. **Arncliffe** is an idyllic village of stone cottages and porched barns arranged around a large oblong green, much in demand as a backdrop for the long-running Yorkshire 'soap' *Emmerdale*. Charles Kingsley wrote part of *The Water Babies* here, though the book is set largely in Malhamdale. The church commemorates local men-at-arms who fought and died at Flodden Field in 1513.

Head up Ribblesdale on the B6479 towards Horton-in-Ribblesdale. ④

Retrace your route down the B6479 to Stainforth, then turn left on the road signed for Halton Gill. Continue over open moorland to Littondale. ⑤

Head south east on unclassified roads to join the B6160 near Kilnsey. ⑥

Clockwise from far left:
path to Malham Cove;
Arncliffe, Littondale;
waterfall, Horton-in-
Ribblesdale; Malham Cove

Clockwise from above:
Burnsall; Bolton Priory,
Bolton Abbey

Continue south on the
B6160 and east on the
⑦ B6265 into **Grassington**.

Head south east on the
B6265/B6160 from
Grassington as far
⑧ as **Burnsall**.

Take a left-hand turn on an
unclassified road to Apple-
treewick, then follow signs
to **Parcevall Hall Gardens**,
just beyond the next
⑨ village of Skyreholme.

Head north to the B6265
and turn right for Pateley
Bridge. After a couple of
miles you will see **Stump
Cross Caverns**, signed to
your right.

6 KILNSEY

A remarkable natural feature marks this Wharfedale
village. As the largest overhang in Britain, **Kilnsey Crag**
presents an irresistible challenge to intrepid rock-
climbers, who cling to its underside like insects. This
limestone spur juts some 9m (30ft) from the valley
wall, and is one of the country's toughest climbs. If this
level of adrenaline isn't for you, head for **Kilnsey Park**,
where there is a trout farm, nature trails and other
family attractions. **Coniston**, just across the river, has
another strange rock formation resembling a steak-
and-kidney pie with a pastry funnel in its middle.

7 GRASSINGTON

Wharfedale's principal touring centre is a neat and
gentrified little town of cobbled alleys and well-
groomed Georgian buildings. The streets are liberally
sprinkled with teashops and rustic hostelries. The
riverside setting adds much to its charm, and the
Grasswood Nature Reserve on its outskirts makes a
pleasant escape from summer crowds. One of the
national park's main information centres at Colvend is
a useful place to find out about the local area. Nearby
Linton on the opposite bank to Grassington is a quieter
place with classical almshouses and an ancient church.

8 BURNSALL

The view of Burnsall's arched bridge straddling the
River Wharfe has captivated many Dales visitors. The
village's summer sports day and ancient fell-race up a
neighbouring hill attracts a large crowd in August. In
St Wilfred's churchyard stand Viking gravestones and
the village stocks. Look out for a headstone to the
Dawson family, carved by the renowned sculptor Eric
Gill. The village benefited greatly from the generosity of
Sir William Craven, a local worthy who was twice made
Lord Mayor of London. He funded several projects such
as the lovely bridge and the village school.

9 PARCEVALL HALL GARDENS

Enjoying grandstand views from a hillside setting,
these extensive woodland gardens with skillfully
planted rockeries and shrubberies are worth seeking
out. The Elizabethan mansion isn't open to the public,
but tearooms and picnic areas take advantage of an
outstanding panorama over Wharfedale. To the south, a
high fell called Simon's Seat (485m, 1591ft) adds a scenic
craggy backdrop.

10 STUMP CROSS CAVERNS

These show-caves were discovered by lead miners in the mid-19th century. The intricate passageways were formed by underground watercourses, and contain impressive stalagmite and stalactite formations. Ancient fossilised bones of long-extinct reindeer, bison and wolverines have also been unearthed here. Unusually, you can visit the caves without a guide.

11 PATELEY BRIDGE

This attractive little market town, winner of many Britain-in-Bloom contests and plentifully stocked with cafes and shops, is another popular stop-off for visitors. Though it's well outside the national park, it makes the perfect base for exploring Nidderdale to the north (*see below*). The much-loved **Nidderdale Museum** in the former workhouse will fill you in on local history and customs. At the top of the high street on Old Church lane, the ruined church of **St Mary** is set in a pretty churchyard. Just outside the town is the Water Mill Inn, where an old flax mill has been restored to working order.

12 BRIMHAM ROCKS

These natural outcrops of gritstone in a high moorland setting of heather and bilberries have been worn into fantastic shapes by wind and weather. Many bear fanciful names – the Anvil, the Castle, the Sphinx and so forth. The sculptor Henry Moore said their influence on his childhood imagination helped to mould the strong, abstract forms typical of his work. The rocks are scattered over an extensive site owned by the National Trust.

13 BOLTON ABBEY

Given the name of the village, it's a bit confusing to discover that the atmospheric Wharfeside ruins here correctly belong to **Bolton Priory**. The building dates from 1154, and was founded by an Augustinian community that grew immensely wealthy on the proceeds of local sheep. Parts of the church, chapter house, cloisters and prior's lodging can still be seen. Immortalised by Turner in 1809 and restored by Pugin in the late 19th century, this lovely site now forms part of the Yorkshire estate of the dukes of Devonshire. It is predictably well kept with excellent visitors' facilities. A memorable woodland walk leads upstream to the **Strid**, where the river surges through a narrow crevice. The banks here are just 2m (6ft) apart – close enough to tempt a leap, but a missed foothold on the slippery rocks means almost certain death in the ferocious currents below. To cross the river more safely, use the stepping stones near the ruined priory. About three miles north east of Bolton Abbey is **Barden Tower**, a curious folly-like building that began life as a medieval hunting lodge. It was renovated by the redoubtable Lady Anne Clifford (*see p14*), who restored Skipton Castle after the Civil War, and who spent the last part of her life at Barden Tower. It now serves as a guesthouse and restaurant.

Continue along the B6265 into ***Pateley Bridge***. ⑪

Take the B6165 south east out of town and turn off to the left after a mile or so, following signs to ***Brimham Rocks***. ⑫

Return to the B6165 and head south east, forking right on to the B6451 at Dacre Banks. Continue as far as the A59 and turn right towards Skipton. ***Bolton Abbey*** *is signposted to the right on the B6160.* ⑬

Continue north along the B6160 and turn left to return to ***Skipton*** *on local roads via Eastby.*

 ❶

WITH MORE TIME

From Pateley Bridge, head up a minor road to Nidderdale *(left)*, an Area of Outstanding Natural Beauty. Beyond the Gouthwaite Reservoir lies a weird ravine of caverns and pot-holes called How Stean Gorge, with overhanging cliffs and dripping vegetation. It's spooky enough to have been chosen as a location setting for science fiction dramas such as *Doctor Who* or *Blake's Seven*. These strange landforms were carved over millennia by the How Stean Beck on its descent from upper Nidderdale.

Richmond and the picture-postcard northern Dales

Two famous dales, Wensleydale and Swaledale, are the star attractions of this part of England. Studded with charming settlements and encased in beautiful scenery, they provide enough scope and interest for a stay of several days. But the minor sidetracks up lesser-known dales can be just as rewarding – all the more so once you escape the crowds and have this glorious countryside all to yourself.

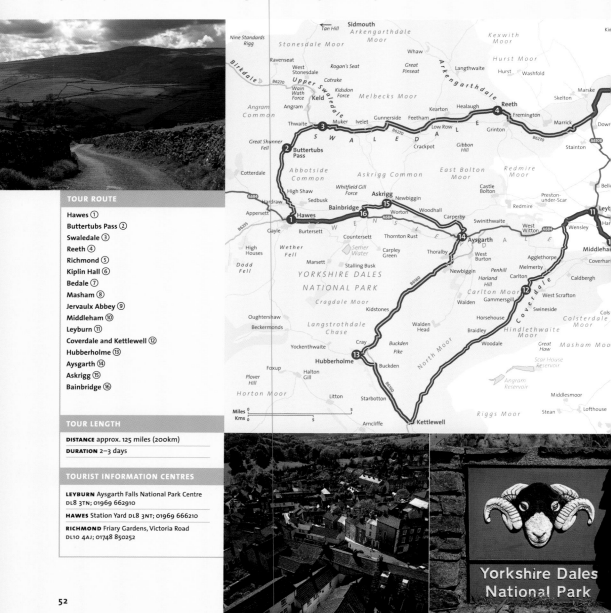

TOUR ROUTE

Hawes ①
Buttertubs Pass ②
Swaledale ③
Reeth ④
Richmond ⑤
Kiplin Hall ⑥
Bedale ⑦
Masham ⑧
Jervaulx Abbey ⑨
Middleham ⑩
Leyburn ⑪
Coverdale and Kettlewell ⑫
Hubberholme ⑬
Aysgarth ⑭
Askrigg ⑮
Bainbridge ⑯

TOUR LENGTH

DISTANCE approx. 125 miles (200km)
DURATION 2–3 days

TOURIST INFORMATION CENTRES

LEYBURN Aysgarth Falls National Park Centre
DL8 3TN; 01969 662910

HAWES Station Yard DL8 3NT; 01969 666210

RICHMOND Friary Gardens, Victoria Road
DL10 4AJ; 01748 850252

Clockwise from far left: view of the Dales; Swaledale; Hardraw Force, Hawes; Druid Temple, Masham; national park sign; Richmond town centre

1 HAWES

Appropriately enough, Wensleydale's principal town is the main outlet for its most famous product – cheese. You'll find this in abundance at its lively Tuesday market stalls, and also at the Wensleydale Creamery on Gayle Lane (*see p54*). A less well-known Hawes industry is demonstrated at the Hawes Ropemaker, former premises of W R Outhwaite & Son, the last traditional twine firm in town. Hand-made specialist products (dog-leads, skipping ropes, leading reins) are made in a purpose-built workshop. In the old railway station opposite is the **Dales Countryside Museum**, covering 10,000 years of local history with exhibitions on typical crafts and trades such as peat-cutting, lead-mining and knitting. Just out of town is **Hardraw Force**, one of England's highest single-drop waterfalls (best after heavy rainfall). You can walk behind the cascade on a rocky ledge.

Head north out of Hawes on unclassified roads towards Thwaite, pausing at the Green Dragon pub to walk to Hardraw Force before reaching Buttertubs Pass. ②

2 BUTTERTUBS PASS

High on the remote fells between Wensleydale and Swaledale are the strange rock formations known as the Buttertubs, where yawning fissures eroded by rushing streams have left flat-topped, circular pillars of limestone. In the past, farmers traversing this high pass (518m, 1,700ft) on their way to market would pause here for a breather, and dangle their dairy produce in these potholes to keep cool. The depths of some of them reach an impressive 30m (100ft).

Continue north on unclassified roads to Thwaite, and turn right on to the B6270 along Swaledale. ③

53

Keep going east
along the B6270
as far as **Reeth.**

3 SWALEDALE

Visitors encounter a scene of pastoral tranquility in this dale, whose most numerous inhabitants seem to be its sturdy sheep (*see p55*). The landscapes here are very ancient: the villages of Thwaite and Muker have Norse names dating back to Viking days. Old stone barns known as laithes are dotted around the valley, and the long-established meadows are ablaze with a rich tapestry of wild flowers from springtime onwards. In the 18th and 19th centuries, however, Swaledale was the heart of a thriving lead-mining industry. The remains of old smelting houses, crushing mills and rusty-grey spoil-heaps can still be seen around Gunnerside Gill, where streams were dammed to scour out the ore.

Swaledale is less widely visited than some other Yorkshire Dales, but is no less beautiful or interesting, and all the more enjoyable for being less crowded. Lovely walks lead along the bucolic valley floor and up into the wild fells to either side.

Clockwise from far right: views of Richmond Castle; Thwaite, Swaledale

WENSLEYDALE CHEESE

The first cheese in Wensleydale was reputedly made by medieval monks, originally from sheep's milk. Following the Dissolution, the recipe changed and by the 1840s the sweet, crumbly cows'-milk version we know today was well established. The first commercial dairy was founded in Hawes at the beginning of the 20th century, and the Wensleydale Creamery is now a firm fixture on the tourism trail, much boosted recently by the well-known dietary preference of Nick Park's animated cartoon characters Wallace and Gromit. Cheese-making tours show you how it is made, after which you can sample and purchase a variety of white or blue-veined Wensleydale cheeses. It is sold in bandaged truckles or waxed miniatures, smoked or mixed with chives, cranberries, apricots – even papaya and mango. Whatever next, Gromit?

4 REETH

Swaledale's largest settlement, dominated by its sloping village green, has a prosperous, upmarket air. With its national park information centre and plenty of craft shops and cafes, Reeth is a natural base for walks or tours up Arkengarthdale (see p59). The **Swaledale Folk Museum** contains an eclectic array of bits and bobs connected with bygone lifestyles. Just south east of Reeth is **Grinton**, whose church was for centuries the only one in Swaledale. Coffins were carried many miles along a rough track known as the Corpse Way to be buried here. Just east of Reeth stand the ruined priories of Marrick and Ellerton near the banks of the Swale. Ellerton dates from the 15th century and was orginally a Cistercian house. The tower and nave still stand.

5 RICHMOND

Yorkshire's Richmond is very different from its Surrey namesake, but it is just as full of civic pride, amply justified by its magnificent setting and admirable state of preservation. This Dales gateway is indeed a jewel, crammed with historic buildings that surround an enormous cobbled square. The splendid **castle** looming above the River Swale on a rocky outcrop dates from Norman times and is still largely intact as it saw very little military action. Behind its curtain walls lie England's oldest Great Hall and a keep over 30m (100ft) high. A heritage garden reflects the castle's lengthy past, and a walk beneath the walls gives a fine prospect of the river. Just off the market place is another noteworthy building, the authentically Georgian **Theatre Royal** dating from 1788. The exquisitely restored interior and a small museum can be visited. Displays on local crafts and a reconstruction of a medieval cruck house are among the items on show at the **Richmondshire Museum**, and the town's regimental associations are emphasized at the **Green Howards Regimental Museum** in a collection of more than 3,000 medals and bloodstained pistols. Army personnel are still much in evidence in Richmond due to the large garrison at nearby Catterick. There is a pleasant riverside walk to the 12th-century ruins of **Easby Abbey** on the south east edge of town.

Continue along the B6270 east until you reach the A6108, turning left for *Richmond*.

Leave Richmond via the B6271 towards Brompton-on-Swale. On the east side of the A1, you'll find signs to *Kiplin Hall*.

Retrace your route along the B6271 and join the A1 at Catterick. Head south down the A1 to Leeming Bar, then turn west on to the A684 to Bedale.

6 KIPLIN HALL

Not far from Bolton-on-Swale, Kiplin Hall was built in the early 1620s as a hunting lodge for George Calvert, secretary of state to James I, later the first Lord Baltimore and the founder of Maryland, USA. Its design, unique in Jacobean architecture, uses mellow red brick instead of Yorkshire stone to construct a tall, compact, symmetrical, country house with central domed towers on each side of a pavilion. The interior has a great deal of Victorian influence, although there are some fine Georgian fireplaces and an 18th century staircase, which leads to a series of domestic rooms and the Long Gallery. Paintings by G F Watts and Angelica Kauffman adorn the dining room walls, while watercolours by Lady Waterford fill the decorative sitting room.

7 BEDALE

Another ancient market town, Bedale first gained its charter in 1251, and its market cross dates from the 14th century. The **Church of St Gregory** dominates the wide main street, the clock on its tower curiously off-centre. It contains a bell rescued from nearby Jervaulx Abbey after the Dissolution. Also on the main street, the Georgian mansion of **Bedale Hall** provides handsome premises for the tourist information centre with its fine plasterwork and 'flying' staircase. Just south of Bedale, **Thorp Perrow Arboretum** is a fine assembly of rare specimen trees, including national collections of ash, lime and walnut. It is especially attractive when the spring bulbs are out, or when the leaves turn in autumn. You can see birds of prey being put through their paces at its on-site falconry centre. Nearby Snape Castle dates from 1426. Katherine Parr, widow of one of the Neville family who owned it, lived here for ten years before becoming Henry VIII's sixth and final wife.

Continue south along the B6268 turning right on the A6108 to the village of Masham.

8 MASHAM

For the uninitiated, this place is pronounced 'Mazzam', but among real ale fans, it needs little introduction. Masham is the home of two famous breweries, **Theakstons** and its rival the **Black Sheep Brewery** (set up by an independent-minded family member when Theakstons was taken over by Scottish and Newcastle in 1989). Both produce excellent ales: Theakstons Old Peculier is a legendary brew but some claim Black Sheep is even better. Both also offer tours and tastings. Beer-drinking aside, Masham is a fine little town of dignified Georgian buildings around a typical Dales-style square, livelier than usual on market days (Wednesday and Saturday), and during its traditional September sheep fair. South west of Masham stands a startling Stonehenge lookalike known as the Druid's Temple. This scaled-down replica is no Neolithic antiquity but a folly commissioned by local landowner William Danby in the 1820s.

Take the A6108 north west from Masham, turning off right for Jervaulx Abbey after about 6 miles.

→ • • • • • • • • • • • 9

Clockwise from far left:
Bedale church; castle ruins,
Middleham; ruins of Jervaulx
Abbey; beer barrels, Masham

9 JERVAULX ABBEY

In a romantically untamed setting, the ruins of this monastery are entwined with clambering ivy and surrounded by wild flowers. Founded in 1156, Jervaulx was a Cistercian community like the grander abbeys of Rievaulx and Fountains to the south east. In its heyday, Jervaulx owned most of Wensleydale, and the monks here are believed to be the ones to have made the first Wensleydale cheese (see p54). Identifiable features include the Night Stairs, by which the monks reached the church from their dormitory to attend services in the small hours. The last abbot of Jervaulx was hanged at Tyburn for his vociferous opposition to the Dissolution.

10 MIDDLEHAM

Middleham has several claims to fame. Most obvious is its imposing Norman **castle** where Richard III spent a happy childhood and honeymoon days before his dubious accession to the throne. The castle contains a replica of the famous Middleham Jewel, a magnificent gold and sapphire pendant dating from the late 15th century, discovered here in 1985. The original is now kept in York. Local racehorse training stables give Middleham the soubriquet 'Newmarket of the North'. A castellated bridge crosses the River Ure here, and like most Dales towns, it has a large cobbled market place surrounded by Georgian buildings.

11 LEYBURN

Two major roads converge at this modest agricultural town on the edge of the national park, making it the principal gateway to Wensleydale from the east. Leyburn is a major auction centre for antiques, and has several unusual visitor attractions. One is the **Teapottery**, a self-explanatory craft workshop where a weird and wonderful range of tea-drinking equipment is on sale. Another is a violin-making studio, where visitors are welcome. Two interesting gardens can be viewed nearby. East of Leyburn, **Constable Burton Hall** gardens surround a handsome Georgian house, while at Coverham (near Middleham), **Forbidden Corner** is an intriguing walled garden with secret passages and joky statues. The neighbouring village of **Wensley**, after which the dale was originally named, was all but wiped out in an outbreak of the plague in 1563. Its 13th-century church of Holy Trinity is one of the most impressive anywhere in the Dales, the choir-stalls elaborately carved with poppies.

*Continue north along
the A6108 as
far as **Middleham**.*

*Drive another couple of
miles north on the A6108
into **Leyburn**. Turn left here
for the A684 and Wensley.*

*Just beyond Wensley, turn
left off the A684 on local
roads south into **Coverdale**.*
➔ • • • • • • • • • • • • 12

Clockwise from above:
Kettlewell; Bainbridge;
Aysgarth Falls

13 HUBBERHOLME

The delightful 13th-century **church** of Hubberholme famously contains the ashes of author J B Priestley. It has a Norman tower, a rare rood-loft dating from 1558, and pews carved by 'Mouseman' Robert Thompson of Kilburn. Look for the mouse carvings – his family firm's trademark. Hubberholme is the meeting point of Wharfedale and the much less well-known Langstrothdale, an ancient hunting forest now extensively planted with conifers.

14 AYSGARTH

After heavy rainfall, the **Aysgarth Falls**, just to the east of town, make a memorable sight. Here the River Ure tumbles over a series of low waterfalls at one of the best-loved beauty spots of the Dales. Inevitably, it can get very crowded in high summer. The peaty falls (called Upper, Middle and Lower) are reached by a path from the car park, and extend along about half a mile of the river's course. Aysgarth itself has a fine church with a 16th-century screen rescued from Jervaulx Abbey. The **Yorkshire Museum of Carriages**, housed in an old mill, displays a collection of Victorian vehicles, including a hansom cab, a charabanc and an old milk-float. A short detour northwards takes you to the doughty fortress at **Castle Bolton**, an estate village stretching along a single street. The 14th-century fortifications were built by Sir Richard Scrope from Masham. Mary Queen of Scots spent a six-month stretch here. Huge towers and dungeons survive the centuries, but have been empty since 1645. Fine views and medieval gardens add to its appeal.

12 COVERDALE AND KETTLEWELL

This easterly tributary of Wensleydale is a quiet and gentle valley enjoyably off the beaten tourist trail. The upper reaches meander over a high pass alongside lonely sheep farms and the grand fells of Whernside. **Kettlewell**, at the southern end of the Coverdale road, is back in Wharfedale again, here a U-shaped valley liberally laced with dry stone walls. These days Kettlewell makes a charming walking base, but its old lead-miners' cottages and smelting mills indicate it was not always such a rural retreat. During the late 18th and early 19th centuries it was something of an industrial boomtown.

Turn north on to the B6160 at Kettlewell and follow the River Wharfe through Starbotton and Buckden, then detour briefly left through Hubberholme.

Return to the B6160 and head northwards, following signs to Aysgarth.

To avoid the busy A684, take unclassified roads along Wensleydale to Askrigg.

15 ASKRIGG

After Wensley's sudden decline from a plague outbreak in the 16th century, Askrigg became the main Dales trading centre for the clock-making, brewing and textile industries. However, the railway age transferred Askrigg's prosperity to Hawes, where Wensleydale's station was built. But Askrigg's largely unchanged historic buildings later became an unexpected source of revenue. During the 1980s this unspoilt little market town provided a location setting for the popular TV series *All Creatures Great and Small*, based on the stories of Thirsk vet James Herriot. 'Skeldale House' is still on the tourist trail, but many other elegant streamside houses and the 15th-century church are worth a look.

16 BAINBRIDGE

Here, as at Ripon, an ancient horn-blowing ceremony takes place each evening at 9pm during the winter months. It is said the tradition goes back to Norman times, and was intended to guide travellers to safety through the lonely forests that once surrounded this idyllic village. The broad, sloping green still has its stocks, and a restored corn mill now produces hand-made doll's houses. The low hill visible above the roofs is a glacial drumlin, once the site of a Roman fort. To the south, **Semer Water** is an Ice Age lake created when a retreating glacier dammed the River Bain.

Take local roads south towards the A684 and Bainbridge. **16**

Drive west along the A684 back to Hawes. **1**

WITH MORE TIME

Explore the upper reaches of **Swaledale**, and its tributary valley **Birkdale**, running towards the Cumbrian border. The fast-flowing Swale rises on moorland north of the village of **Keld**, where Britain's highest pub (the Tan Hill Inn at 528m, 1,732ft) stands on old drover's roads, actually the meeting point of three counties. Both the Pennine Way *(left)* and the Coast-to-Coast Path pass through Keld. Arkengarthdale is another picturesque side-valley off Swaledale, once known for lead-mining. Strange place-names like Whaw and Booze may arouse your curiosity.

Whitby and the magic of the North York Moors National Park

Tucked within the folds of the wild moorland landscape of the North York Moors lie picturesque villages and the impressive ruins of abbeys and priories, such as Mount Grace, Rosedale and Rievaulx, glorious reminders of the heydays of the monasteries. But it is the ruins of Whitby's 7th-century abbey perched on the headland overlooking the harbour that perhaps enjoys the most dramatic setting of them all.

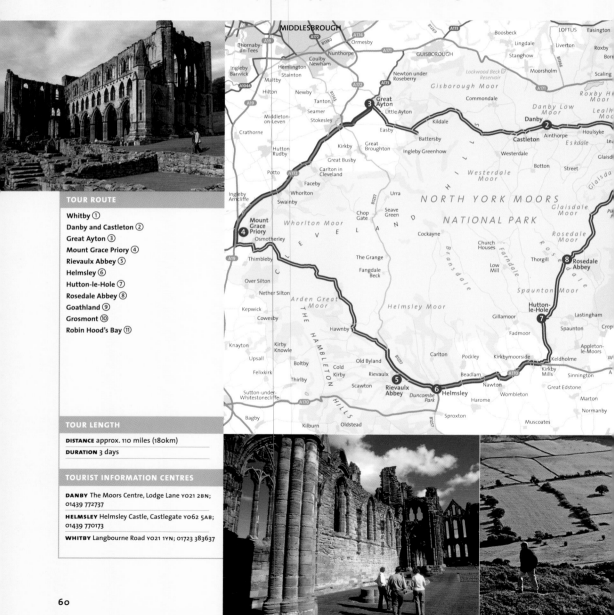

TOUR ROUTE

Whitby ①
Danby and Castleton ②
Great Ayton ③
Mount Grace Priory ④
Rievaulx Abbey ⑤
Helmsley ⑥
Hutton-le-Hole ⑦
Rosedale Abbey ⑧
Goathland ⑨
Grosmont ⑩
Robin Hood's Bay ⑪

TOUR LENGTH

DISTANCE approx. 110 miles (180km)

DURATION 3 days

TOURIST INFORMATION CENTRES

DANBY The Moors Centre, Lodge Lane YO21 2BN; 01439 772737

HELMSLEY Helmsley Castle, Castlegate YO62 5AB; 01439 770173

WHITBY Langbourne Road YO21 1YN; 01723 383637

Clockwise from far left:
Rievaulx Abbey; Whitby;
North York Moors;
Whitby Abbey

1 WHITBY

The coastal town of Whitby has a unique, old-world charm with its skyline dominated by the ruins of the 7th-century **abbey** and its maze of alleyways and narrow streets that tumble down to the busy quayside below. From the old town at East Cliff, 199 steps lead up to Whitby's parish church, **St Mary's**, one of the finest examples of Anglo-Saxon architecture in the country, featuring 17th-century carved pews made by ship's carpenters and craftsmen. Its sinister-looking churchyard inspired Bram Stoker to write the Gothic novel *Dracula*. Whitby has provided a safe haven to fishing fleets for centuries, and it was once the main whaling port for northern England. A whalebone arch now commemorates this industry. This seafaring town became well known for its connections with the 18th-century explorer Captain James Cook and the father-and-son whaling masters of the Scoresby family. Today Whitby, with its higgledy-piggledy arrangement of red-roofed houses and attractive buildings on the steep slopes of the River Esk, is a delight to explore.

*Leave Whitby on the A171
west and then take local
roads through Eskdale to
Danby and on to Castleton.*

②

2 DANBY AND CASTLETON

Danby is best known for the national park's **Moors Centre**, an excellent place to find out about local walks and places of interest. The building was originally a shooting lodge for the Dawnay family, who ruled the roost hereabouts. It stands in terraced waterfront grounds, where an arched packhorse bridge called the Duck Bridge crosses the River Esk. The now ruined **Danby castle** dates from the 14th century, and was once the home of Katherine Parr, the sixth and luckiest wife of Henry VIII (who survived him). As its name suggests, **Castleton** once had a castle too, but all that remains is a grassy mound. Much of the stone is believed to have been pillaged for the castle at Danby. The Esk Valley Walk begins at Castleton, and follows the river all the way to the coast at Whitby. From Castleton Rigg, you can take a footpath route to Ralph Cross, the national park emblem at the head of Rosedale.

*From here continue on
unclassified roads west
cross country via Battersby
and Little Ayton
to Great Ayton.*

③

Take the A173 south to its junction with the A172 at Stokesley and then follow this south to reach the A19. Take the A19, south looking for a signpost on your left to **Mount Grace Priory**.

Cut across country on unclassified roads east via Osmotherley and Hawnby to the B1257. Continue south for a few miles and then turn right on local roads to **Rievaulx Abbey**.

3 GREAT AYTON

The unassuming village of Great Ayton, overlooked by the conical hill Roseberry Topping, is in a conservation area. With a fine prospect of the Cleveland Hills escarpment to the south, it has two centres, High and Low Green, which are linked by the River Leven. The village once boasted a thriving textile and tanning industry but today it is popular stop on the Esk Valley Railway, which runs from Whitby to Middlesbrough. Great Ayton is best known for its most famous son, Captain James Cook, who spent the early part of his life here. The Cook family home on Bridge Street was built by James' father in 1755, though in 1934 it was dismantled and shipped to Australia, where it now stands in Melbourne's Fitzroy Gardens. A granite obelisk now marks the original site of Cook's cottage in Great Ayton.

ROSEBERRY TOPPING

Blow the cobwebs away by taking a leisurely walk up this conical hill. The peculiar shape is due to a geological fault and a mine that collapsed early in the 20th century. From the summit there is a magnificent 360-degree view that allows you to see as far as Teeside in one direction and the Yorkshire Dales in another. Newton and Cliff Ridge Woods skirt the northern edge of the hill, and Cliff Rigg quarry still retains evidence of the extraction of whinstone, once used for roadbuilding. The area is rich in wildlife, particularly moorland birds.

4 MOUNT GRACE PRIORY

Tucked neatly into the wooded western edge of the Cleveland Hills, the atmospheric ruin of Mount Grace Priory is one of the finest examples of a 14th-century Carthusian monastery. Typically, Mount Grace housed 15 or so hermit-monks living as solitaries in two-storey, 7m-sq cells (22sq-ft). The ground floor had a fireplace and a wooden staircase to the room above. Each also had a small garden, separated from the next by high walls, in which the monk worked alone. Meeting their fellows only for matins and vespers, and the occasional feast day when services were held in the church, the monks would spend ten hours each day in their cells, reading, praying, eating and meditating. Now in the guardianship of English Heritage, little remains of the priory, save for its gatehouse and church, a small herb garden, and a reconstructed and furnished cell, enabling you to experience the austere conditions in which the monks lived.

5 RIEVAULX ABBEY

In a deep valley by the River Rye, Rievaulx Abbey is celebrated for the beauty and tranquillity of its setting. It was founded in the 12th century as the first Cistercian outpost in the north, and intended to be a mission centre from which the 'white monks' could spread across the country. Indeed, by the 13th century the influence of Rievaulx had spread to no fewer than 19 other abbeys in the north of England, prospering largely thanks to sheep-farming as well as an active patronage of culture. Rievaulx's fortunes changed in the late 13th century, when the abbey suffered severe financial problems, war, famine and plague, and was later destroyed during the Dissolution of the monasteries. The austere and impressive ruins include extensive remains of the church, once one of the finest in the region, and cloistral buildings of which five arches survive.

Close by you will find the **Rievaulx Terrace and Temples**, a grassy terrace, bright in springtime and early summer with wild flowers, and an outstanding 18th-century landscape garden that also contains two mid-18th-century temples. Intended as a banqueting house, the Ionic temple has beautiful painted ceilings and fine furniture. From the garden's elevated position you get a fine view of the abbey ruins and over Ryedale below.

6 HELMSLEY

Helmsley's undulating red rooflines, honey-coloured buildings, market square, beautiful riverside walks, chintzy tea rooms and genteel country pubs have lost none of their fascination. Almost every view of this market town is dominated by the tall ruin of its **castle**, which dates from the 12th century and was once home to the Duke of Buckingham, court favourite of Charles I. It was severely damaged during the Civil War, but the nearby Tudor mansion survived largely intact.

Most people come to visit the fine baroque mansion of **Duncombe Park**, which has been, in turn, the Duncombe's family seat for nearly 300 years, a hospital, and a girls' school until it was re-occupied in 1985 by Lord Feversham. He restored the mansion and opened it to the public in 1990. The well-preserved, early 18th-century landscaped gardens are classically English and surrounded by parkland. You can wander at leisure across the great lawn and terraces, amid temples, yew trees and woodland walks, and the scented 'secret garden' surrounding the old conservatory. **Helmsley Walled Garden**, originally developed to supply produce to the Duncombe estate, lay abandoned until 1994, when a major restoration programme was initiated to bring the site back into life as a fully working kitchen garden, now open to the public.

Clockwise from above:
Rievaulx Abbey; Helmsley town and castle; Roseberry Topping outside Great Ayton; Mount Grace Priory

Continue past Rievaulx and rejoin the B1257 to **Helmsley** *and locally signed roads to Duncombe Park* ⑥

Follow the A170 east for 7 miles, and then leave it for local roads north to **Hutton-le-Hole**.
⑦

⊕ From Hutton-le-Hole
  follow unclassified roads
⑧ north to **Rosedale Abbey**.

⊕ Continue on local roads
  north from Rosedale Abbey,
  heading for Egton Bridge;
  but before reaching the
  village, turn right using
  more unclassified roads
⑨ south to **Goathland**.

⊕ Follow unclassified roads
  north down to **Grosmont**
⑩ and Eskdale.

Take unclassified roads east
to reach the B1416. Turn
right for 3 miles to the
junction with A171. Then go
left for 1 mile before using
local roads east to descend
to **Robin Hood's Bay**.

→ • • • • • • • • • • ⑪

7 HUTTON-LE-HOLE

Tucked neatly into the southern edge of the North York Moors National Park, the village of Hutton-le-Hole centres around a beautiful village green. Nearby, the open-air **Ryedale Folk Museum**, very much a 'hands-on' experience, depicts 4,000 years of North Yorkshire life in the form of reconstructed historic buildings including shops, thatched cruck cottages, an Elizabethan manor house, barns and workshops.

8 ROSEDALE ABBEY

Gloriously set on the heather-covered moors flanking the River Severn, the tiny, eponymous village of Rosedale Abbey retains just a hint of its industrial past, most noticeable in cottages built of bluish ironstone brick. In 1328, Edward III granted permission to the nuns of Rosedale Abbey to work the ore here, but 500 years later it was considered poor quality and worthless and production ceased. In the 19th century, however, Rosedale ore was discovered to be magnetic and of the highest quality. Five millions tons were extracted in 20 years, and in 1861 the Rosedale Ironstone Railway was constructed to carry the iron to the furnaces of Teeside. By the 1920s, the seams had worn thin and a depression was looming, presaging the final end of the mining operations here. Little remains of the original abbey except a stone pillar and a remnant staircase, though a good deal of the stonework went into building the village church. The ironstone railway tracks now serve to help walkers to enjoy the wider landscapes of the moors.

9 GOATHLAND

Despite its undoubtedly beautiful setting, few would visit the village of Goathland were it not for television. For it was here that many of the scenes of the series *Heartbeat*, set in the fictional village of Aidensfield, were filmed. Many of the series' landmarks are recognisable, including the village store, the offices of the garage/funeral director, the public house and, of course, the railway station, which is actually on the line of the North York Moors Railway. In a narrow wooded dell nearby is **Mallyan Spout**, a 21.5-m high waterfall (70ft) that is especially dramatic when the water is low and only a thin flow of water cascades down like at mystical veil.

10 GROSMONT

Grosmont (pronounced grow-mont) is set in a bucolic landscape of scattered fields and farms, and attracts hikers on the Coast-to-Coast Walk (*see p65*). But the village had a more gritty past as the hub of a thriving ironstone industry, and it is its railway and industrial heritage that attracts visitors today. In 1836, the building of one of the railway lines exposed a rich seam of ironstone of the highest quality, which was transported by rail to the coast at Whitby. The presence of the railway still features largely in the everyday life of the village, as it is the northern terminus of the North York Moors Railway (*see p65*). From Grosmont you can also enjoy easy walks across the adjacent moorland, in particular to the **Low Bridge Stones**, a small group of ancient stones on the edge of Goathland Moor.

COAST-TO-COAST WALK

Originally devised by Alfred Wainwright, the
Coast-to-Coast Walk crosses northern England
from St Bees Head in Cumbria to Robin Hood's
Bay on the Yorkshire coast. A great swathe of
the route runs from Richmond, across the Vale
of Mowbray and onto the Cleveland Hills that
form the northern escarpment of the North
York Moors, before descending to tease a route
through the villages of Eskdale as it heads for
journey's end at Robin Hood's Bay.

11 ROBIN HOOD'S BAY

Legend has it that Robin Hood found a quiet bay on
the edge of the North York Moors and decided it would
make an ideal retreat. Here, under the name of Simon
Wise, he returned time and time again, keeping a small
fleet of fishing boats, which he used to put to sea
whenever danger threatened. The village that bears his
name was once a fishing community, with a not
insignificant sideline in smuggling: now it has caught
the imagination of tourists, and is a popular holiday
resort. Its red-roofed houses and shops are perched
precariously at, or above, the water's edge, many so
small and narrow that they have a 'coffin window'
above the door to enable coffins, too large to be passed
down the narrow staircases, to be removed from
upstairs rooms. At high tide the sea runs into the
village street, and at low tide the Scars, or rocks, run far
out to sea and are full of rock pools.

*Clockwise from above:
Robin Hood's Bay; North York
Moors Railway, view
from Goathland*

*Leave Robin Hood's Bay
along the B1447 north to
rejoin the A171 and follow
this north back to **Whitby**.*

WITH MORE TIME

The **North Yorkshire Moors Railway** was originally opened in 1836 as a horse-
drawn tramway running from Whitby to Pickering. It was closed in 1965 but was
resurrected by the North Yorkshire Moors Preservation Society, reopening in
1973. Operating throughout the year (though not every day) the railway line is
run as a living museum. The trains travel through delightful scenery of wooded
valleys and heather-clad moorland, and visit isolated villages where you can
alight and walk or cycle across the moors.

Stately homes in the Vale of York

The vales of York and Mowbray form a wide plain bordered by the Yorkshire Dales to the west, the hills of the North York Moors to the north and the Yorkshire Wolds to the east. This fertile region is dominated by rolling farmlands, but at its centre lies the vibrant city of York, known for its magnificent minster and its historic buildings. The Vale of York is also rich in stately homes, priories and abbeys, but the jewel in the crown is one of England's grandest houses, the striking Castle Howard.

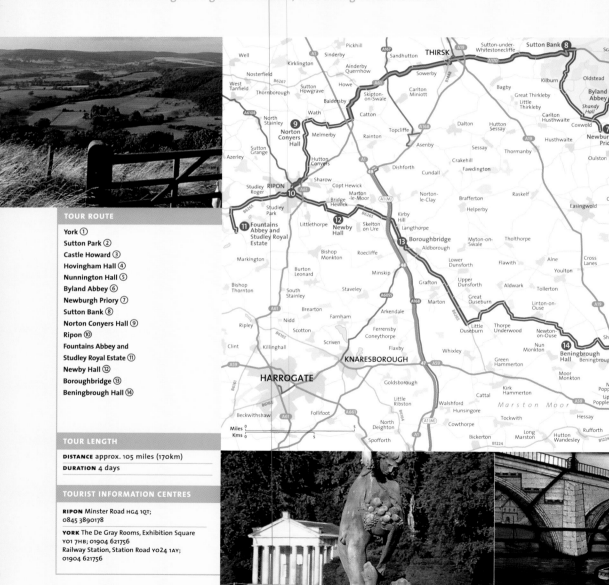

TOUR ROUTE

York ①
Sutton Park ②
Castle Howard ③
Hovingham Hall ④
Nunnington Hall ⑤
Byland Abbey ⑥
Newburgh Priory ⑦
Sutton Bank ⑧
Norton Conyers Hall ⑨
Ripon ⑩
Fountains Abbey and
Studley Royal Estate ⑪
Newby Hall ⑫
Boroughbridge ⑬
Beningbrough Hall ⑭

TOUR LENGTH

DISTANCE approx. 105 miles (170km)
DURATION 4 days

TOURIST INFORMATION CENTRES

RIPON Minster Road HG4 1QT;
0845 3890178

YORK The De Gray Rooms, Exhibition Square
YO1 7HB; 01904 621756
Railway Station, Station Road YO24 1AY;
01904 621756

Clockwise from far left:
Sutton Bank; Castle Howard;
York Minster; stained glass,
Merchant Adventurers' Hall,
York; Studley Royal Estate

1 YORK

The fascination of York lies in the many layers of history that are reflected by the varied architecture and museums to see here. Almost 2,000 years ago the Roman Ninth Legion set up a small fort at Eboracum, strategically positioned on the River Ouse. This in turn became the Saxon stronghold of Eorforwick. And so it remained until 866 when the town was seized by the Vikings. Within 10 years Jorvik – as it was called – became the Viking capital and evolved into one of the most viable trading ports in Northern Europe. In the mid-11th century the last great king was killed. The Normans then fortified the city, and began work on the minster in 1220, on the site of the Roman headquarters. York flourished as the medieval wool trade expanded, under the direction of the monastic settlement. When this influence declined following the Dissolution, so, too, for a time, did the prominence of the city. During the 18th century, York became a fashionable social centre, and witnessed the building of many fine Georgian buildings. The railway, opened in 1839, and the city boomed. York's many highlights reflect the city's key periods of history.

*Leave York north west to the junction with the A19. Turn right on the A1237 (the ring road), and turn left onto the B1363, continuing to Sutton-on-the-Forest and **Sutton Park**.*

➔ • • • • • • • • • • 2

67

YORK MINSTER

The largest Gothic cathedral in northern Europe, York's
magnificent **minster** is an amazing medieval
architectural achievement that took more than 250
years to build. Founded in AD627 by King Edwin of
Northumbria, it is dedicated to St Peter. The minster is
deservedly renowned for its glorious stained-glass
windows, 128 in all, justifying the claim that York
houses more than half of Britain's finest stained glass.
The huge Great East Window is a prime example, the
largest stained glass window in the world, created in
the early 15th century by John Thornton of Coventry.
Energetic visitors can climb the central tower's 275
steps to be rewarded with an incredible view of the
countryside around the city, and, in good weather, the
spire of Lincoln Cathedral, more than 60 miles away.

YORK'S SIGHTS

The **Jorvik** centre leads visitors on a journey through
York in Viking times at the end of the first millennium,
and is one of the most popular attractions in Britain. It
was inspired by the finds from an archaeological dig in
the city between 1976 and 1981.

Built on Roman foundations, York has the best-
preserved medieval **city walls** in England, interspersed
with with gateways and towers. Most of the walls are
intact and can be followed on a rampart walk
extending over two miles. The network of lanes and
alleyways collectively known as **The Shambles** is
arguably Europe's best preserved medieval centre. The
streets are so narrow in some places, you can touch
both sides. The stunning, timber-framed **Merchant
Adventurers' Hall** on Fossgate reminds one what
craftsmanship went into medieval building. It is one of
the largest buildings of its kind and date, and yet was
built in 1357–61, before most of the craft or trade guild
halls in Britain were formed.

York's Georgian history is revealed in **Fairfax House**
on Castlegate, one of the finest mid-18th-century
townhouses in England. It typifies the best of rococo
decoration, with ornate stucco ceilings, and is home to
the fine Noel Terry collection of furniture. The **Treasurer's
House** is a stunningly beautiful, 18th-century
townhouse. Originally home to the treasurers of York
Minster and built on a Roman road (the ghosts of a
Roman legion reputedly march through the cellars), the
house was designed by John Carr and displays fine
period furniture, porcelain and clocks.

The **National Railway Museum**, the largest in the world,
houses an extensive collection of locomotives, rolling
stock, railway equipment and documents, and traces
the history of the railway from the Rocket to Eurostar.

2 SUTTON PARK

Located in the tranquil village of Sutton-on-the-Forest, Sutton Park is a private residence but opens its doors to the public. This elegant early Georgian house contains exquisite examples of hand-painted Chinese-influenced wallpaper and a wonderful collection of porcelain including Meissen and Sèvres. Here you can enjoy a stroll in the gardens overlooking spacious parkland thought to have been designed by Meikle, a follower of 'Capability' Brown.

3 CASTLE HOWARD

The breathtaking Castle Howard is still home to the family whose forebears conceived, designed, and built it more than 300 years ago. Set dramatically between two lakes, this palatial 18th-century stately home, designed by Sir John Vanbrugh, is one of England's most beautiful and grand historic houses. It has unrivalled collections of furniture, paintings, porcelain and statuary gathered by generations of the Howard family. All the rooms have knowledgeable guides on hand to relate the family history and stories about the building itself. You may even meet costumed guides posing as Sir John Vanburgh; Frederick, 5th Earl of Carlisle, an avid collector; Georgiana, the 6th Countess of Carlisle; or even housemaid Ann Tibbles. In the chapel three embroidered panels are from a set of eight by William Morris, representing Lucretia, Hippolyte and Helen of Troy (they were made into the oak-framed screen for the 9th Countess). However, at the heart of the house, the Great Hall is the most palatial room of all with its cupola rising an incredible 22m (70ft).

The grounds are every bit as spectacular as the house. Vanburgh's influence continues here, with many vistas dotted with pyramids, towers and obelisks, including the commanding Temple of the Four Winds originally constructed simply as a place to rest and eat. The Mausoleum, best viewed from Temple Hole Basin, is still the burial place of the Howard family and is virtually the size of a palace in its own right.

4 HOVINGHAM HALL

For more than 400 years Hovingham Hall has been the family seat of the Worsleys, an old Lancashire family. This gorgeous Palladian house was built between 1750 and 1770 by Thomas Worsley to his own design and is unique in being entered through The Riding School. Thomas Worsley was passionate about horses and architecture; the house remains the product of the extraordinary fusion of these two obsessions.

5 NUNNINGTON HALL

This mellow, honey-coloured manor house set on the banks of the River Rye was once home to the doctor of Henry VIII, Edward VI and Elizabeth I. From the magnificent oak-panelled hall, three staircases lead to the family rooms: the nursery, the haunted room and the attics with their fascinating Carlisle collection of miniature rooms, which are fully furnished to represent different periods. Outdoors, the totally organic walled-garden retains a lovely 17th-century character with delightful mixed borders, orchards of traditional fruit varieties, spring-flowering meadows and a collection of 50 different types of clematis.

Head north east using unclassified roads via Sheriff Hutton to Castle Howard. **3**

Continue north on local roads to meet the B1257, and turn left for Hovingham Hall. **4**

Head north on the B1257 and turn right along unclassified roads to Nunnington Hall. **5**

Take local roads west to briefly return to the B1257, leaving it at Oswaldkirk to take unclassified roads west to Byland Abbey. **6**

From Byland Abbey take unclassified roads to the nearby **Newburgh Priory**.

Return north on local roads to the A170, and cross the main road for **Sutton Bank**.

Return to the A170 west towards Thirsk, and continue along the A61 Then follow unclassified roads across the A1 west to **Norton Conyers**.

Follow local roads south to briefly rejoin the A61 and turn right for **Ripon**.

Take the B6265 west out of Ripon and follow unclassified roads to reach **Fountains Abbey and Studley Royal Estate**.

6 BYLAND ABBEY

This beautiful ruin, set in the shadow of the Hambleton Hills, was once one of the great northern monasteries, rivalling Rievaulx (*see p63*) and Fountains (*see p71*) in importance. A truly outstanding example of early Gothic architecture, it originally had a wheel window on the west front that inspired the design for the Rose Window in York Minster (*see p68*). Its splendid collection of medieval tiles, remarkably still in situ, is the second largest in Europe.

7 NEWBURGH PRIORY

Lying in a fold in the hills near the ancient village of Coxwold, Newburgh Priory is an elegant stately home. Founded in 1145 and built on the site of an earlier Augustinian priory, it is a confusing mish-mash of medieval, Tudor, Jacobean and Georgian architecture. The entrance is probably medieval and leads to the former manorial court rooms, including the Black Gallery and Justice Room, brightly painted in contrast to the dark panelling of the entrance. Newburgh is the reputed burial place of Oliver Cromwell, whose remains – possibly minus his head – were said to have been brought here by his daughter Mary when she married the second Viscount Fauconberg. However, tradition dictates that the tomb is never to be opened. You can wander the extensive grounds or venture into the walled garden to admire the skilfully designed topiaried yews.

8 SUTTON BANK

The steep escarpment of Sutton Bank is a splendid vantage point at the edge of the Hambleton Hills and the North York Moors, offering extensive views over the Vale of York and the Vale of Mowbray. Landmarks include Whitestone Cliff and Roulston Scar, the former overlooking the picturesque Lake Gormire. Close by are the peaceful villages of Sutton-under-Whitestonecliff, and Kilburn, famous for the White Horse designed by Thomas Taylor, a native of Kilburn, and cut in 1857.

9 NORTON CONYERS HALL

Norton Conyers is a mid-14th-century house with Tudor, Stuart and Georgian additions, and has been the home of the Graham family since 1624. Its elegant Dutch gables, which top each of the main façades, date from then. The interior contains some elegant 17th- and 18th-century furniture. The Great Hall is hung with splendid family portraits by Romney and Batoni, and paintings of hunting scenes, while the long table was almost certainly made in the late Middle Ages. However, Norton is best known for its association with Charlotte Brontë. She visited the house in 1839 and was told of the legend of a mad woman who had been incarcerated in one of the gable rooms. When Charlotte wrote *Jane Eyre* eight years later, she almost certainly had the mad woman in mind when she created Mrs Rochester, and Norton Conyers as the basis for Mr Rochester's house, Thornfield Hall.

10 RIPON

Ripon – the 'Cathedral City of the Dales' – is one of England's smallest cities. The huge market place is surrounded by an interesting mix of buildings of differerent, but mainly Georgian, architectural styles and eras. It is dominated by a 28m-high (90-ft) obelisk that has been used by the official red-coated horn blower to sound the 'setting of the watch' every day at 9pm for the last 1,000 years.

Today's **cathedral** is the fourth building to have stood on this site. Its great glory is the Saxon crypt – all that remains of an early stone church – less than 3m (10ft) high and 2m (7ft) wide. Architecturally, the cathedral is a mishmash of styles but the Early English west front, added in 1220, is one of the finest in England.

Clockwise from above:
Studley Water Garden;
statuary, Ripon cathedral;
Byland Abbey

11 FOUNTAINS ABBEY AND STUDLEY ROYAL ESTATE

Declared a World Heritage Site in 1987, Fountains Abbey is the National Trust's most visited site. The large estate contains the remains of a fine Cistercian abbey, ten historic buildings including a Victorian church, a medieval deer park and elegant ornamental lakes. The **abbey**, founded in 1132, was one of the nation's richest and most influential in the 13th century. It burned down in 1539 towards the end of the Dissolution of the monasteries; but all was not entirely lost for much of the masonry from the abbey went into building the nearby Elizabethan **Fountains Hall**. Today the abbey is Britain's largest monastic ruin.

John Aislabie inherited the Studley estate and devoted himself to the creation of the garden we see today. The **Water Garden** is arguably England's most important 18th-century example with its formal geometric design and wonderful vistas. It drew its inspiration from the great French landscape gardeners of that era but retained a remarkable individuality. The **Deer Park** is the oldest part of the estate, and is still home to 500 red, fallow and Sika deer as well as temples, follies and statues requisite of gardens of this period.

Return to the B6265, follow this east through Ripon and then take unclassified roads south to **Newby Hall**.

Clockwise from above: exterior, Newby Hall; gardens, Beningbrough Hall; tapestry room, Newby Hall; aerial view, Newby Hall

12 NEWBY HALL

To the south east of Ripon, on the banks of the River Ure, red-brick Newby Hall was built in the style of Sir Christopher Wren in the 1690s. In the 1760s William Weddell, an ancestor of Richard Compton, the present owner, made the Grand Tour of Europe, returning with many works of art including a set of Gobelin tapestries and superb classical statuary that required a grand setting. Robert Adam, the foremost classical architect of the period, was commissioned by Weddell to adapt the hall to exhibit his collection: he designed the Entrance Hall, Library, domed Sculpture Gallery and Tapestry Room. The latter survives in its entirety and shows Adam's skill in creating harmony between the decoration of a room and its furnishings, which among other things feature a fine collection of Chippendale furniture. The gardens at Newby Hall – a series of close-knit rectangles – were influenced by Lawrence Johnston's famous garden at Hidcote, and have lovely double herbaceous borders, backed by yew hedges that sweep down to the River Ure. Each year Newby displays a different selection of contemporary sculpture throughout the woodland, orchard and gardens. Around 50 to 60 works in a variety of media including wood, bronze, stone, glass and steel are usually on show.

From Newby Hall return to the B6265 south east to **Boroughbridge**.

→ • • • • • • • • • • • ⑬

13 BOROUGHBRIDGE

This former coaching stop on the Great North Road is now bypassed by the A1 motorway, but it is worth visting to investigate a curious trio of gritstone pillars just outside the town. The Devil's Arrows, as they are popularly known, measure as much as 7m (22ft) in height, and are believed to date back to the early Bronze Age. Just outside the exceptionally pretty Georgian village of Aldborough is an ancient Roman settlement at a fording point along the River Ure. Isurium Brigantium was the capital of the Brigantes, the largest tribe in Roman Britain and was where the Ninth Legion established camp. A stretch of wall and two well-preserved mosaic pavements can be seen.

14 BENINGBROUGH HALL

The symmetrical red-brick front of this stunning Georgian mansion is breathtaking. Built in 1716, the house possesses one of the finest Baroque interiors in England. The formality of early 18th-century life at Beningbrough is reflected in the ground-floor setting of state bedrooms with intimate 'closets' in which visiting guests could receive friends in privacy. Throughout, there is elegant wood panelling and carving, most noticeable in the drawing room. More than 100 portraits on loan from the National Portrait Gallery decorate many of the walls, and on the first floor an unusual central corridor runs along the house from end to end.

Beningbrough also has a fully equipped Victorian laundry that gives a fascinating insight into the drudgery of servants' lives at that time. The walled garden is delightful and the surrounding parkland with its interesting wooden sculptures worth exploring.

*Head south on the B6265 and take unclassified roads east to **Beningborough Hall.***

*Continue east, using local roads, to join the A19, and follow this south back to **York**.*

WITH MORE TIME

Eden Camp *(left)* near Malton, created in an original World War II prisoner of war camp, offers a chance to experience life during those perilous years. Each of the 33 huts, built by Italian POWs, has a unique theme like woman at war, all designed, through sight, sound and smell, to portray the reality of wartime existence. By contrast **Wharram Percy** is the best-known of 3,000 medieval villages in Britain that were simply abandoned between the 11th and 18th centuries. You can still see the foundations of more than 30 simple houses, and the ruins of the church.

Gazetteer

The dramatic hills and dales of eastern Lakeland

Acorn Bank Garden and Watermill
Temple Sowerby, nr Penrith CA10 1SP
Tel: 017683 61893
www.nationaltrust.org.uk

Appleby Castle
Appleby-in-Westmoreland CA16 6XH
Tel: 017683 53823
www.cumbria-the-lake-district.co.uk

Brough Castle
Church Brough, Brough,
Kirkby Stephen CA17 4EJ
www.english-heritage.org.uk

Carlisle Castle
Carlisle CA3 8UR
Tel: 01228 591922
www.english-heritage.org.uk

Carlisle Cathedral
7 The Abbey, Carlisle CA3 8TZ
Tel: 01228 548151
www.carlislecathedral.org.uk

Dalemain House and Gardens
Dalemain, Penrith CA11 0HB
Tel: 017684 86450
www.dalemain.com

Patterdale Hall
Glenridding, nr Penrith CA11 0PT
Tel: 017684 82233
www.patterdalehall.org.uk

Penrith Castle
Castlegate, Penrith CA11 7HX
www.english-heritage.org.uk

Rheged – The Village in the Hill
Redhills, Penrith CA11 0DQ
Tel: 01768 868000
www.rheged.com

Tullie House Museum and Art Gallery
Castle Street, Carlisle CA3 8TP
Tel: 01228 534781
www.tulliehouse.co.uk

The rugged fells of the western Lakeland

Cockermouth Castle
Not open to the public
Cumberland Pencil Museum
Southey Works, Greta Bridge,
Keswick CA12 5NG
Tel: 017687 73626
www.pencils.co.uk

Honister Slate Mine
Honister Pass, Borrowdale CA12 5XN
Tel: 017687 77230
www.honister-slate-mine.co.uk

Howk Bobbin Mill
Calderdale
www.visitcumbria.com

Lakeland Sheep and Wool Centre
Egremont Road, Cockermouth CA13 0QX
Tel: 01900 822673
www.sheep-woolcentre.co.uk

Maryport Maritime Museum
1 Senhouse Street, Maryport CA15 6AB
Tel: 01900 813738
www.thecumbriadirectory.com

Maryport Steamship Museum
South Quay, Maryport CA15 8AB
Tel: 01900 815954
www.thecumbriadirectory.com

Mirehouse
Keswick CA12 4QE
Tel: 017687 72287
www.mirehouse.com

Senhouse Roman Museum
The Battery, Sea Brows, Maryport CA15 6JD
Tel: 01900 816168
www.senhousemuseum.co.uk

Wordsworth House
Main Street, Cockermouth CA13 9RX
Tel: 01900 820884
www.nationaltrust.org.uk

The charms of southern Lakeland

Abbot Hall Art Gallery and Museum of Lakeland Life
Abbot Hall, Kendal LA9 5AL
Tel: 01539 722464
www.abbothall.org.uk

Beatrix Potter Gallery
Main Street, Hawkshead LA22 0NS
Tel: 015394 36355
www.nationaltrust.org.uk

Brantwood
Coniston LA21 8AD
Tel: 015394 41396
www.brantwood.org.uk

Cartmel Priory
The Square, Cartmel,
Grange-over-Sands LA11 6QB
Tel: 015395 36874
www.nationaltrust.org.uk

Dove Cottage and the Wordsworth Museum
Grasmere LA22 9SH
Tel: 015394 35544
www.wordsworth.org.uk

Furness Abbey
Barrow-in-Furness LA13 0TJ
Tel: 01229 823420
www.english-heritage.org.uk

Grizedale Forest Visitor Centre
Grizedale Forest, Hawkshead LA22 0QJ
Tel: 01229 860010
www.forestry.gov.uk

Hill Top
Near Sawrey, Hawkshead,
Ambleside LA22 0LF
Tel: 015394 36269
www.nationaltrust.org.uk

Holker Hall and Gardens and Lakeland Motor Museum
Cark-in-Cartmel, nr Grange-over-Sands LA11 7PL
Tel: 015395 58328
www.holker-hall.co.uk

Levens Hall
Kendal LA8 0PD
Tel: 015395 60321
www.levenshall.co.uk

Muncaster Castle
Ravenglass CA18 1RQ
Tel: 01229 717614
www.muncaster.co.uk

Rydal Mount and Gardens
Rydal, nr Ambleside LA22 9LU
Tel: 015394 33002
www.rydalmount.co.uk

Sizergh Castle
Sizergh, nr Kendal LA8 8AE
Tel: 015395 60951
www.nationaltrust.org.uk

Steamboat Museum
Rayrigg Rd, Bowness, Windermere LA23 1BN
Tel: 015394 45565
www.visitcumbria.com

Lancaster and the rural uplands of the Forest of Bowland

Ashton Memorial and Williamson Park
Lancaster LA1 1UX
Tel: 01524 33318
www.williamsonpark.com

Carnforth Station Visitor Centre
Warton Road, Carnforth LA5 9TR
Tel: 01524 735165
www.carnforth-station.co.uk

Clitheroe Castle
Castle Hill, Clitheroe BB7 1BA
Tel: 01200 424568
www.lancashire.gov.uk

Ingleborough Cave
Clapham LA2 8EE
Tel: 015242 51242
www.ingleboroughcave.co.uk

Lancaster Castle
Shire Hall, Castle Parade, Lancaster LA1 1YJ
Tel: 01524 64998
www.lancashire.gov.uk

Leighton Hall
Carnforth LA5 9ST
Tel: 01524 734474
www.leightonhall.co.uk

Leighton Moss Nature Reserve
Leighton Moss, Nr Carnforth
Tel: 01524 701601
www.rspb.org.uk

White Scar Caves
Ingleton LA6 3AW
Tel: 01524 242244
www.whitescarcave.co.uk

THE UNEXPECTED ATTRACTIONS OF
LANCASHIRE'S COASTAL PLAIN

Astley Hall Museum and Art Gallery
Astley Park, Chorley PR7 1NP
Tel. 01257 515927
www.chorley.gov.uk

Camelot Theme Park
Charnock Richard, Chorley PR7 5LP
Tel: 01257 453044
www.camelotthemepark.co.uk

Formby Point Squirrel Reserve
Victoria Road, Freshfield L37 1LJ
Tel: 01704 878591
www.nationaltrust.org.uk

Harris Museum and Art Gallery
Market Square, Preston PR1 2PP
Tel: 01772 905410
www.visitpreston.com

Marshside RSPB Nature Reserve
Nr Southport
Tel: 01704 536378
www.rspb.org.uk

Martin Mere Wildfowl and Wetlands Trust
Between Ormskirk and Southport
Tel: 01704 895181
www.wwt.org.uk

National Football Museum
Sir Tom Finney Way, Deepdale
Preston PR1 6RU
Tel: 01772 908400
www.nationalfootballmuseum.com

Pleasureland Southport
Marine Drive, Southport PRB 1RX
Tel: 08702 200205
www.pleasureland.uk.com

Rufford Old Hall
Rufford, nr Ormskirk L40 1SG
Tel: 01704 821254
www.nationaltrust.org.uk

Wigan Pier
Wallgate, Wigan WN3 4EU
Tel: 01942 323666
www.wlct.org

WEST YORKSHIRE'S BRONTË COUNTRY

Betty's Cafe Tea Rooms
1 Parliament Street, Harrogate HG1 2QU
Tel: 01423 877300
Crag Lane, Beckwithshaw,
Harrogate HG3 1QB
Tel: 01423 505604
www.bettys.co.uk

Bramham Park
Bramham, Wetherby LS23 6ND
Tel: 01937 846000
www.bramhampark.co.uk

The Brontë Parsonage Museum
Church Street, Haworth BD22 8DR
Tel: 01535 642323
www.bronte.org.uk

Chevin Forest Park
Otley
www.leeds.gov.uk

Cliffe Castle Museum
Spring Gardens Lane, Keighley BD20 6LH
Tel: 01535 618231
www.bradfordmuseums.org

East Riddlesden Hall
Bradford Road, Keighley BD20 5EL
Tel: 01535 607075
www.nationaltrust.org.uk

1853 Gallery
Salts Mill, Shipley, Saltaire BD18 3LB
Tel: 01274 531185
www.saltsmill.org.uk

Gibson Mill
Hardcastle Crags Estate Office, Hollin
Hall, Crimsworth Dean, Hebden Bridge
HX7 7AP
Tel: 01422 844518
www.nationaltrust.org.uk

Harewood House
Harewood, Leeds LS17 9LQ
Tel: 0113 218 1010
www.harewood.org

Harry Ramsden's
Otley Road, Guiseley, Leeds LS20 8LZ
Tel: 01943 874641
www.harryramsdens.co.uk

Keighley and Worth Valley Railway
The Railway Station, Haworth,
Keighley BD22 8NJ
Tel: 01535 645214
www.kwvr.co.uk

Kirkstall Abbey
Abbey Road, Kirkstall, Leeds LS5 3EH
Tel: 0113 230 5492
www.leeds.gov.uk

Lotherton Hall and Gardens
Aberford, Leeds LS25 3EB
Tel: 0113 281 3259
www.leeds.gov.uk

Manor House Museum and Art Gallery
Castle Yard, Church Street, Ilkley LS29 9DT
Tel: 01943 600066
www.bradfordmuseums.org

Mercer Art Gallery
Swan Road, Harrogate HG1 2SA
Tel: 01423 556130
www.harrogate.gov.uk

**National Museum of Photography,
Film and Television**
Bradford BD1 1NQ
Tel: 0870 7010200
www.nmpft.org.uk

Ripley Castle and Gardens
Harrogate HG3 3AY
Tel: 01423 770152
www.ripleycastle.co.uk

**Royal Pump Rooms Art Gallery and
Museum**
Crown Place, Harrogate HG1 2RY
Tel: 01423 556188
www.harrogate.gov.uk

Stockeld Park
Wetherby LS22 4AW
Tel: 01937 586101

Turkish Baths
Royal Baths, Parliament Street,
Harrogate HG1 2WH
Tel: 01423 556746
www.harrogate.gov.uk

**Victorian Reed Organ and
Harmonium Museum**
Victoria Hall, Victoria Road,
Saltaire Village, Shipley BD18 4PS
Tel: 01274 585601
www.thisisbradford.co.uk

THE NATURAL WONDERS OF THE SOUTHERN DALES

Bolton Priory
Bolton Abbey, Skipton BD23 6EX
Tel: 01756 718009
www.boltonabbey.com

Craven Museum
Town Hall, High Street, Skipton BD23 1AH
Tel: 01756 706407
www.cravendc.gov.uk

Kilnsey Park
Kilnsey, nr Skipton BD23 5PS
Tel: 01756 752150
www.kilnseypark.co.uk

Nidderdale Museum
King Street, Pately Bridge HG3 5LE
Tel: 01756 752780
www.nidderdalemuseum.com

Parcevall Hall Gardens
Skyreholme, Skipton BD23 6DE
Tel: 01756 720311
www.parcevallhallgardens.co.uk

Skipton Castle
Skipton BD23 1AW
Tel: 01756 792422
www.skiptoncastle.co.uk

Stump Cross Caverns
Greenhow Hill, Pateley Bridge,
Harrogate HG3 5JL
Tel: 01756 752780
www.stumpcrosscaverns.co.uk

Watershed Mill and Visitor Centre
Langcliffe Road, Settle BD24 9LR
Tel: 01729 825539
www.watershedmill.co.uk

**Yorkshire Dales Falconry and
Conservation Centre**
Crows Nest, nr. Giggleswick, Settle LA2 8AS
Tel : 01729 822832
www.yorkshiredales.org

RICHMOND AND THE PICTURE-POSTCARD NORTHERN DALES

Bedale Hall
North End, Bedale DL8 1AA
Tel: 01677 423797
www.hambleton.gov.uk

Black Sheep Brewery
Wellgarth, Masham, Ripon HG4 4EN
Tel: 01765 689227
www.blacksheepbrewery.com

Constable Burton Hall
Leyburn DL8 5LJ
Tel: 01677 450428
www.constableburtongardens.co.uk

Dales Countryside Museum
Station Yard, Hawes DL8 3NT
Tel: 01969 667450
www.yorkshiredales.org.uk

Easby Abbey
nr Richmond
www.english-heritage.org.uk

Forbidden Corner
The Tupgill Park Estate, Coverdale
Middleham, Leyburn DL8 4TJ
Tel: 01969 640638
www.yorkshiredales.org.uk

Green Howards Regimental Museum
Trinity Church Square,
Richmond DL10 4QN
Tel: 01748 825 611
www.greenhowards.org.uk

Jervaulx Abbey
Jervaulx, Ripon HG4 4PH
Tel: 01677 460226
www.jervaulxabbey.com

Kiplin Hall
Nr Scorton, Richmond DL10 6AT
Tel: 01748 818178
www.kiplinhall.co.uk

Middleham Castle
Middleham DL8 4QR
Tel: 01969 623899
www.english-heritage.org.uk

Richmond Castle
Richmond DL10 4QW
Tel: 01748 822493
www.english-heritage.org.uk

Richmondshire Museum
Ryders Wynd, Richmond DL10 4JA
Tel: 01748 825 611
www.richmond.org.uk

Swaledale Folk Museum
Reeth Green, Reeth, nr Richmond DL11 6QT
Tel: 01748 884373
www.yorkshiredales.org.uk

Thorp Perrow Arboretum
Bedale DL8 2PR
Tel: 01677 425323
www.thorpperrow.com

Yorkshire Museum of Carriages
Yore Mill, by Aysgarth Falls,
Wensleydale DL8 3SR
Tel: 01748 823275

WHITBY AND THE MAGIC OF THE NORTH YORK MOORS NATIONAL PARK

Duncombe Park
Helmsley, York YO6 5EB
Tel: 01439 772625
www.duncombepark.com

Helmsley Castle
Helmsley YO62 5OB
Tel: 01439 770442
www.english-heritage.org.uk

Helmsley Walled Garden
Cleveland Way, Helmsley YO62 5AH
Tel: 01439 771427
www.helmsleywalledgarden.org.uk

Moors Centre
Danby, Whitby YO21 2NB
Tel: 01439 772737
www.redcar-cleveland.gov.uk

Mount Grace Priory
Staddle Bridge, Northallerton DL6 3JG
Tel: 01609 883494
www.nationaltrust.org.uk

North Yorkshire Moors Railway
Pickering Station, Pickering YO18 7AJ
Tel: 01751 472508
www.nymr.demon.co.uk

Rievaulx Abbey
Rievaulx YO62 5LB
Tel: 01439 798228
www.english-heritage.org.uk

Rievaulx Terrace and Temples
Rievaulx, Helmsley YO62 5LJ
Tel: 01439 798340
www.nationaltrust.org.uk

Ryedale Folk Museum
Hutton-le-Hole, York YO62 6UA
Tel: 01751 417 367
www.ryedalefolkmuseum.co.uk

Whitby Abbey
Whitby YO22 4JT
Tel: 01947 603568
www.english-heritage.org.uk

Stately homes in the Vale of York

Beningbrough Hall
Beningbrough, York YO30 1DD
Tel: 01904 470666
www.nationaltrust.org.uk

Byland Abbey
nr Coxwold, YO61 4BD
Tel: 01439 748283
www.english-heritage.org.uk

Castle Howard
York YO60 7DA
Tel: 01653 648444
www.castlehoward.co.uk

Eden Camp
Malton YO17 6RT
Tel: 01653 697777
www.edencamp.co.uk

Fairfax House
Castlegate, York YO1 9RN
Tel: 01904 655543
www.fairfaxhouse.co.uk

Fountains Abbey and Studley Royal Estate
Fountains, Ripon HG4 3DY
Tel: 01765 608888
www.nationaltrust.org.uk

Hovingham Hall
Hovingham, York YO62 4LU
Tel: 01653 628771
www.hovingham.co.uk

Jorvik
Coppergate, York YO1 9WT
Tel: 01904 643211
www.jorvik-viking-centre.co.uk

Merchant Adventurers' Hall
Fossgate, York YO1 9XD
Tel: 01904 654 818
www.theyorkcompany.co.uk

National Railway Museum
Leeman Road, York YO26 4XJ
Tel: 01904 686286
www.nrm.org.uk

Newburgh Priory
Coxwold, York YO61 4AS
Tel: 01347 868372
www.newburghpriory.co.uk

Newby Hall
Ripon HG4 5AE
Tel: 0845 4504068
www.newbyhall.co.uk

Norton Conyers Hall
Ripon HG4 5EQ
Tel: 01765 640333
www.historichouses.co.uk

Nunnington Hall
Nunnington, nr York YO62 5UY
Tel: 01439 748283
www.nationaltrust.org.uk

Ripon Cathedral
Ripon HG4 1QS
Tel: 01765 602072
www.riponcathedral.org.uk

Sutton Park
Sutton-on-the-Forest, York YO6 1DP
Tel: 01347 810249
www.statelyhome.co.uk

Treasurer's House
Minster Yard, York YO1 7JL
Tel: 01904 624247
www.nationaltrust.org.uk

Wharram Percy Deserted Medieval Village
Wharram le Street
www.english-heritage.org.uk

York Minster
York YO1 7JF
Tel: 01904 557216
www.yorkminster.org

Index

Credits

t = top; tl= top left; top centre = tc; top right = tr; centre = c; bottom = b; bottom left = bl; bottom centre = bc; bottom right = br

VisitBritain would like to thank the following for their assistance with photographic material for this publication:

Rod Edwards jacket

Cumbrian Tourist Board 11c, 11c, 21b, 22t, 24t; **Lancashire County Development Ltd** 31b, 34b, 36b, 38c; **NTPL/Ian Shaw** 73t; **Yorkshire Tourist Board** 51b, 73b

All remaining photographs have been sourced from VisitBritain's online picture library (www.britainonview.com) with credits to:
Dave Ashwin 35t; Sally Devine 39t; Rod Edwards 46b, 49br, 54b, 61t; Graham Evans 12t, 62c; VK Guy/Mike Guy 27b; David Sellman 13t; Duncan Shaw 37t; Richard Watson 17t, 47tr, 48t, 62b, 67t, 71t; Robert Westwood 57; John Whitaker 44tr

Design: Anthony Limerick, Clare Thorpe, Janis Utton

Editorial: Naomi Peck, Debbie Woska

Picture Research: Rebecca Shoben

Publishing: Jane Collinson, Edward Farrow